Shanghai Escape

A HOLOCAUST REMEMBRANCE BOOK FOR YOUNG READERS

Shanghai Escape

KATHY KACER

Second Story Press

Library and Archives Canada Cataloguing in Publication

Kacer, Kathy, 1954-, author
Shanghai escape / Kathy Kacer.

(Holocaust remembrance book for young readers)
Issued in print and electronic formats.
ISBN 978-1-927583-10-4 (pbk.).—ISBN 978-1-927583-11-1 (epub)

1. Holocaust, Jewish (1939-1945)—China—Shanghai—Juvenile fiction.
2. Jewish children in the Holocaust—China—Shanghai—Juvenile fiction.
3. Jews—China—Shanghai—Juvenile fiction. 4. World War, 1939-1945—China—Juvenile fiction.
I. Title. II. Series: Holocaust remembrance book for young readers

PS8571.A33S53 2013   jC813'.54   C2013-903871-X
C2013-903872-8

Edited by Kathryn Cole
Copyedited by Phuong Truong
Designed by Melissa Kaita

*The views or opinons expressed in this book and the context in which the
images are used, do not necessarily reflect the views or policy of, nor imply approval
or endorsement by, the United States Holocaust Memorial Museum.*

Printed and bound in Canada

*Second Story Press gratefully acknowledges the support of the Ontario Arts Council
and the Canada Council for the Arts for our publishing program. We acknowledge
the financial support of the Government of Canada through the Canada Book Fund.*

MIX
Paper from
responsible sources
FSC® C004071

Published by
SECOND STORY PRESS
20 Maud Street, Suite 401
Toronto, ON M5V 2M5
www.secondstorypress.ca

For Lily Toufar Lash — with deep gratitude
And to my children, Gabi and Jake — may you always know only freedom

Introduction

Shanghai, China. What an unlikely destination for European Jews, trying to escape the cruel, anti-Semitic laws that Adolf Hitler and his Nazi party enforced before the Second World War. As more and more Jews sought safe refuge in the 1930s, world leaders came together in France to discuss the issue of what to do about them. The meetings were known as the Evian Conference. Although everyone sympathized with Jewish families who were trying to escape the persecution in Europe, most countries around the world, including Australia, Canada, and the United States, were not willing to offer safe refuge. Shanghai was one place that allowed Jews to enter.

More than twenty thousand Jewish refugees, mostly from Austria and Germany, came to Shanghai between 1937 and 1939. In the early days of their arrival, they established lives that were not all that different from the ones they had left behind in Europe. They opened shops and restaurants; they created theaters and published newspapers; their children attended schools. They lived side by side with their Chinese neighbors in relative freedom. All of this changed after 1941, when Japan attacked the U.S. Navy in Pearl Harbor, Hawaii, and Japan and the United States entered the Second World War.

Japan and China had been at war for many years. By 1937, the Japanese Imperial Army had occupied Shanghai and imposed harsh conditions on the Chinese citizens who lived there. Japan was also an ally of Nazi Germany. After Pearl Harbor, and under pressure from Adolf Hitler, the Japanese government in Shanghai ordered all the Jewish refugees who had arrived there after 1937 to move into a ghetto in an area of the city called Hongkew.

Twenty thousand Jewish refugees joined nearly a hundred thousand poor Chinese citizens who already lived in Hongkew. Conditions there were harsh. There was little food to eat, poor sanitation, rampant disease, and hardly any medication. Jews needed special pass cards to leave the ghetto and to work in other parts of Shanghai, and these permits, issued by the Japanese, were difficult to obtain. At one point, there was even talk that the Japanese authorities were establishing concentration camps off the coast of Shanghai where Jews would be sent and possibly put to death. The Jewish refugees of Hongkew lived with anxiety and uncertainty about their future.

Lily Toufar and her family arrived in Shanghai in 1938, having fled from Vienna, Austria, on the eve of *Kristallnacht,* the "night of broken glass." On that night, hundreds of synagogues in Germany and Austria were looted and ransacked, and thousands of Jews were beaten, arrested, and imprisoned. Shanghai was a strange and unfamiliar place to Lily. But life became even more difficult after her family was forced to move into the Hongkew ghetto in 1941. She, like thousands of other Jewish refugees, endured the difficult living conditions, dirt, disease, and death, always hopeful that the war would end and her family would still be alive.

This is Lily's story.

Foreword

November 8, 1938

Their bags were packed and waiting at the door. Suitcases and boxes leaned against one another like building blocks. Lily stood next to the luggage, watching her mother count the pieces over and over.

"I hope we've got everything," Mom said, in a voice so soft that Lily had to bend forward to hear her.

Why is Mom whispering when there's no one else in the apartment to hear? Lily wondered. *And why is her face so serious?* Mom's eyebrows were drawn so low they nearly touched the top of her lashes. Lily wrapped her jacket closer around her body and shivered. Even though it was only early November, she felt winter beginning to creep into the apartment. Within a month, her city of Vienna would be blanketed with snow. That had always meant Lily could go tobogganing. She loved racing down snow-covered hills with the wind blowing her short reddish curls straight out behind her. But that was before – in winters past. Now she was beginning to wonder if she would ever again see the surrounding hills of Vienna.

"Why can't I take my other toys?" The sound of her voice echoed in the empty hallway.

Mom paused and looked at her daughter. The lines around her eyes softened, and she reached over to brush Lily's hair behind her ear. "I've explained this to you already. Clothes are more important than

Before the war began, Lily lived in Vienna with her Mom and Pop.

dolls, my darling." Lily gazed up at her mother. Mom never wore a smidge of make-up and couldn't have cared less about her appearance. But even now, as she rushed about packing up last minute things, Lily marveled at how nice she still looked, as if she was planning a dinner party and not an escape from their home.

"But you packed my books, didn't you, Mom? We're not leaving those behind."

Her mother nodded. "Yes, Lily. The books you chose are packed here in this box. You see?" she added. "I've written your name on it in black ink."

"What about that?" Lily pointed to Mom's treadle sewing machine – one of the only pieces of furniture that stood amongst the cartons and cases.

Mom paused and then spoke again. "We have no idea what we will find in Shanghai. We have to be prepared with those things that are really necessary. If I'm able to sew, then I can help your father earn money for our family. Now where did I pack the pots?" She turned back to surveying the luggage while Lily slumped against the wall. *Aren't my toys as necessary as Mom's sewing machine?*

Shanghai! It had meant nothing to Lily when Mom told her the name of the city in China they were escaping to; it may as well have been the moon. The only thing she had thought of was Vienna's Prater Amusement Park close to their home where, in the middle of the merry-go-round, stood the statue of the *Calafati*, a Chinese man dressed in colorful clothing. It was huge, maybe ten times Lily's height, and would turn in slow circles as she rode up and down on one of the wooden horses. She wondered if there were giant men like that in Shanghai, a place that was halfway around the world.

"Is it just for a vacation, Mom? Like going to the cottage in the country?" That was the question Lily had asked weeks earlier when the plans were being carefully arranged.

When Lily tried to imagine what Shanghai would be like, all she could think of was the statue of the Calafati, a wooden Chinese man in the center of the merry-go-round that she rode as a child in Vienna.

Her mother had shaken her head. "No, Lily. This time we're leaving for much, much longer." Mom had gone on to explain that they would travel by train to Italy and then by boat to Shanghai. "It will take weeks to get there, perhaps more than a month. But we should be thankful that there's a city anywhere in the world that still allows Jews like us to enter. God knows there aren't many places left that will," she had added.

The sounds of crashing and shattering glass from somewhere outside filled Lily's apartment. Mom, her eyes suddenly wide, moved to the sitting room window and peered out at the dark streets, careful to hide behind the long curtains. Lily followed, curious about the angry cries that rose up from the street below. She could have sworn that she heard a chorus of people shouting "Down with the Jews!" *How is that possible? I must have heard wrong.*

"Lily, get back!" Mom's voice sounded angry as she yanked Lily away from the window, pulling so hard on her arm that Lily cried out. Mom hardly noticed. "It's starting," she said. She turned and ran through the apartment, switching off every light until there was only one left on at the back of the flat. Darkness fell across the luggage, casting long eerie shadows up the door. Mom returned to stand next to her daughter, reaching out to pull her close. Lily's arm was still sore, but she didn't say a word.

"Those Nazi thugs!" Mom practically spat those words out. "They're going to arrest Jewish men across the country. That's why we must escape tonight. As soon as your father gets back, we'll go. He should have been here by now," she added. "I only pray he returns safely…." Her voice trailed off until silence joined the darkness in the apartment.

Escaping from our home? Arresting Jewish men? Lily had little understanding of what it meant. She was too young when the laws and rules restricting the freedom of Jewish citizens had been introduced. Occasionally she overheard bits of conversations between her parents or her aunts and uncles. They talked about how Jews couldn't go to movie theaters or restaurants or the ice-cream parlor. Pop once said that Jews were being kicked on the streets and beaten in parks. For the most part it all seemed unreal to Lily; her parents had protected her from knowing about these awful things so that she wouldn't be afraid. But tonight, when she looked into her mother's face, she could see Mom's hot red cheeks, her creased brow, and the fear that glittered in her eyes, even in the darkened apartment. That was real for Lily.

Shoes scraped across the staircase outside their apartment. A key turned in the lock. Lily sucked in her breath as the door opened. It was Pop.

"Oh, thank goodness!" Mom exclaimed as Lily rushed into her father's open arms.

"No need to worry," Pop said, gently prying Lily's arms from around his waist and bending to face his daughter. "Are you all packed, my darling?"

Lily nodded, pointing to the box with her name on it. "My clothes are in the suitcase. That box has my books." She glanced up at her mother. "And just a couple of toys."

Mom sighed. "Did you get the tickets, Fritz?"

Lily's father nodded and reached into the pocket of his overcoat, carefully removing three long envelopes. "We're lucky that our friend warned me about tonight."

"I'm still not sure I completely trust him," Mom replied, as she reached for the envelopes. "After all, he's a member of the SS. Why would someone from Hitler's own police help us out?"

"He had no choice but to sign up, Erna. He was under pressure to join, and it would have been dangerous for him to refuse. I've told you this before. He doesn't believe all the nonsense that the Nazis are saying about Jews." Lily's father looked tired as he patiently explained this to his wife. There were dark shadows under his eyes and his back was bent as if it was too heavy for him to straighten up. "He was very brave to warn us about the dangers," Pop added. "He could be shot for helping us."

Shot for helping us Jews? Lily didn't understand that part at all.

Mom held the envelopes tightly against her chest. "You were gone so long. Did you have any trouble?"

Pop shook his head. "The line-up for tickets went for several blocks. But ours were waiting for me, as promised."

Howling police sirens filled the air outside along with the sound of more destruction and windows shattering. Pop glanced at the door then back at his wife and daughter. He pulled a handkerchief from his pocket and ran it across his forehead, his hand shaking. It was the first time in Lily's life that she had seen her father look so frightened, and it scared her.

"There's a taxi waiting for us outside. It took a lot to convince the driver to bring me home, especially knowing that we're Jews."

"Will he wait?" Mom asked.

Pop nodded. "I paid him a large sum to bring me back here, and promised him even more when he drops us at the train station. Still, we must hurry before he changes his mind."

Lily tugged on her father's arm. "What about Oma and the others?"

"Your grandmother and your Aunt Nini and Uncle Willi will meet us at the train station," Pop replied. "Your Aunt Stella and Uncle Walter are already in Italy waiting for us. Don't worry, Lily," he repeated. "We're all going to sail to Shanghai together, just as I promised."

"And what about our home?" Lily asked, stubbornly. "Are we all going to come back here? Together?"

Lily watched as her Mom and Pop exchanged glances above her head, just like they always did when they didn't want her to know something. Pop dropped to one knee in front of his daughter and looked into her eyes. "That's a question that I just don't have an answer for." With a deep sigh, he rose and moved toward the luggage. "Let's get the cases downstairs. I'll have the taxi driver help me with Mom's sewing machine. He probably won't be happy about that, either." He muttered this last remark under his breath.

Mom wrapped a scarf around Lily's neck and then one around her own. Lily looked around the apartment, trying to commit every detail to memory; the paintings on the walls, the clock that chimed every hour, and down the hallway, her bedroom with her feather-stuffed comforter and her dolls lined up on the shelf like obedient schoolchildren. She was determined to remember everything on the taxi ride to the train station – memorize everything about the city that she was leaving behind.

Pop placed a box under his arm and grabbed two large suitcases, one in each hand. Mom picked up another two. "It's time," he said.

Lily pulled the scarf tighter around her neck and grabbed her smaller suitcase. Then she followed her parents out the door.

Chapter 1

December 7, 1941

The radio blared out an urgent message, and Lily leaned closer so that she wouldn't miss a word.

> *December 7, 1941, a day that will live in history. The Japanese have just attacked Pearl Harbor.*

She shivered in the iciness of the small apartment. Cold air somehow always managed to find its way through the small door from the balcony, or past every windowpane, no matter how many towels Mom stuffed against them. But what Lily hated more than the cold was the dampness that crept into the walls and through the sweaters that she piled on every morning. It was only December; the worst part of winter in Shanghai still lay ahead. Today it was the ominous news coming from the radio that added to the shivers rippling up and down Lily's spine.

A small brown beetle began its slow walk across the floor of the apartment. It had a long way to go if it was going to reach the other side of the room without being trampled by Lily's family members who had gathered to listen to the radio broadcast.

"This is terrible," Pop said, shaking his head from side to side. "America will have no choice now but to join the war." He reached into his pocket and pulled out a handkerchief, mopping it across his brow. His hand was shaking, and Lily remembered another time, three years earlier, when her father had looked this nervous. This news wasn't good.

"But what will that mean?" Mom asked. "America is such a powerful country. Surely President Roosevelt will have no trouble beating back the Japanese." Mom spoke as she entered the room from the small galley kitchen, carrying a tray laden with teacups. She brushed a stray strand of hair off her forehead and proceeded to pass the tea out to her siblings and their spouses.

Lily's Aunt Stella snorted from her seat at the small table in the middle of the room. "Powerful? How powerful can the Americans be if they didn't see this attack coming?" Aunt Stella was usually the cool and unruffled one in the family. Lily always listened and respected her opinions when she spoke, but she felt a distance from this aunt that she couldn't explain. Stella's husband, Uncle Walter, nodded somberly. He was often quiet at these family gatherings, a nervous man who counted out loud when he became tense. Lily could hear him doing that now, under his breath.

"It's one thing for the war to be in Europe where that maniac, Hitler, is trying to control everything. But America is halfway around the world. How can the war be spreading so far?" This comment came from Lily's other aunt. Of her two aunts, Lily had to admit that Aunt Nini was her favorite and more like a second mother. Aunt Nini was the one who bought Lily special toys and took her for tea in the afternoon. When Aunt Nini had married a year earlier, Lily had been so worried that she and her aunt might lose their special relationship. But that wasn't the case. Lily glanced over at Nini's husband, Poldi. Usually, he loved taking Lily aside and entertaining her with Bible stories. But today, Poldi wasn't saying anything. He sat at the table, head down, fingers pressed to his temple.

Mom continued serving the tea as she spoke. "I wouldn't worry about it so much if it weren't for the fact that the Japanese are right here in Shanghai – right under our noses!"

That part was true. The Japanese army had been patrolling the streets of Shanghai for years, ever since they had conquered parts of China in a battle that was still raging.

"It's what Hitler has wanted all along." Pop continued. "He's friends with that crazy Emperor of Japan, Hirohito. Hitler thinks he

Lily came from a warm and loving family that included
(from left to right) her Aunt Stella, her Oma, her Uncle Walter, and
her Mom and Pop. Lily's Uncle Willi (below) loved to tease her.

16

can conquer all of Europe *and* North America. It's a world war he wants. And he may have gotten it."

This last comment brought the entire conversation to a dead stop.

It was in this tiny one-room flat that so many family events took place, and even though Lily was not yet eight years old, she was always in the center of those activities. Often it was evening tea that brought her relatives over to chat about the news of the day. Sometimes it was for celebrations – Lily's birthday, or one of the Jewish holidays. At those times, family members competed with one another, talking louder and over each other to have the last word, laughing and sharing stories about something that had happened at Nini and Poldi's nightclub, or Stella and Walter's coffee house. The only person missing from the room today was Lily's grandmother. Her Oma had died the previous year, leaving an emptiness in Lily's heart that had been hard to fill.

As if reading Lily's mind, Mom spoke again. "Perhaps it's a good thing that Oma isn't here. This news would have destroyed her."

The mood around the table was solemn as the voice crackled from the radio once more.

Such an attack on American soil will surely bring a counter-attack...President Roosevelt will naturally ask Congress for a declaration of war. There is no doubt that such a declaration will be granted.

Pop stood suddenly and began to pace the length of the room. "That's it, then," he said. "The war has spread around the world."

The little brown beetle was halfway across the floor now. Pop, unaware of its presence, had almost crushed it as he walked from one end of the small flat to the other. Lily found herself rooting for the beetle. She usually hated bugs, and their apartment certainly had plenty of them. But this one was so small and alone. *It isn't hurting anyone*, Lily thought. *Why should we hurt it?* And with that, her mind leapt back in time to when her family had arrived here in Shanghai.

Everyone knew about the war in Europe and the evil Adolf Hitler, who had made life so unbearable for Jewish people. That's why Lily and her relatives had left their homes in Vienna, Austria, three years earlier. They were getting away before they could be arrested and sent to some awful place where Jews were beaten and tortured. And for what? Just for being Jewish. That seemed ridiculous to Lily. In truth, the whole quick escape from Vienna had made little sense to her three years earlier. But now, she saw the wisdom in it.

"If you don't watch out, the ghosts are going to get you."

Lily whirled around to face her youngest uncle, Willi. The other relatives were still deep in conversation around the table. The radio had been turned off and moved to a corner of the room as if they could somehow push the bad news away by not listening.

"Stop it, Willi," Lily said, planting her feet firmly on the floor, hands on her hips. At sixteen years of age, Willi was more like a brother to Lily than an uncle. And nothing seemed to give him more pleasure than scaring her with ghost stories. There was even that time, when they were still in Austria, that Willi had held her "hostage" in front of a tree at the cottage, convincing her that the birds were going to attack her. Even now, Lily's heart beat a bit faster as she thought back to how trapped she had felt until Pop had come to her rescue.

This time, Pop was still talking to her other relatives, and Willi would not let up. "Maybe the ghosts'll get you at night when you're sleeping," he continued waving his fingers in front of Lily's face. "Or they'll sneak up behind you when your back is turned."

"There's no such thing as ghosts!" Lily stared up at her uncle, refusing to let him see that the stories he told really did frighten her. Still, she loved him and was glad he was here. She couldn't help remembering that Willi had barely made it out of Vienna when the family had fled.

The night they were leaving Vienna, Willi had been arrested by the SS. Oma refused to go without him, so she and Aunt Nini stayed behind, promising that they would join the rest of the family once they had managed to get Willi out of jail, though at the time they had no idea how they could bring this about. Lily and the other family members didn't learn the details of Willi's release until much later. In desperation, Nini had turned to a Christian friend who was a lawyer, a man who was sympathetic to the Jews and their situation. He had accompanied Nini to the SS headquarters where Willi was being held.

The lawyer had Willi brought in front of him and shouted, "This young man stole my watch! I'll deal with him now. He comes with me!" With that, he took Willi under the arm and escorted him out of the building. The SS officials were too stunned to do anything. They just watched Willi leave. Shortly after, Willi, Oma, and Nini left Vienna by train, bound for Italy. They boarded the next boat for Shanghai, following Lily, her parents, Stella, and Walter.

Only later did Lily and her family discover that the night they had fled Vienna actually had been given a name. People were calling it *Kristallnacht*, the night of broken glass. Synagogues across Germany and Austria had been destroyed, their windows smashed, and the buildings set on fire. Thousands of Jewish men, including Willi, had been arrested that night, though most were not as lucky as he had been. As Lily stared at her uncle, she was thankful that as much as he annoyed and taunted her, she was glad she hadn't lost him on the journey to China.

Now, Willi leaned forward and whispered in Lily's ear, "This time the ghosts are real. The Nazis may not be coming to get us. But the Japanese will!"

Chapter 2

The beetle disappeared into a tiny hole in the far wall as Lily silently cheered its victory march. Then she pushed her annoying Uncle Willi away and darted through the small door onto the balcony. She leaned over the rail, trying to still the wild beating in her chest.

Down below, the streets of Shanghai had become strangely quiet. The usual swarm of cars, bicycles, and rickshaws going in all directions had disappeared along with the hundreds of thousands of people who lived in the city. Lily wondered if all those families were also sitting in their apartments, listening to their radios, and trying to imagine what might happen. The relative quiet outside was a welcome change from the racket that normally filled the air, climbing to such decibels that Lily often covered her ears with her hands just to be able to think. And thinking is what she tried to do now, away from her relatives who were still arguing inside the apartment, and away from Willi and his grim warnings about ghosts.

She was still trying to figure out who the real bad guys were! She was very clear about the Nazis back in Austria and other European countries. But the Nazis were far away from Shanghai, and Lily had lived here for the last three years believing that she and her family were safe. This talk of the Japanese government as the new enemy was something different. Even though she saw Japanese police on the streets every day, she had never realized that Germany and Japan were allies. That was new information. *How can anyone be friends with Nazi Germany!* But if Germany and Japan were friends, and the government of Germany was intent on torturing Jews, did that mean that the Japanese army here in Shanghai would begin to terrorize families like hers, too? That was the question that worried Lily most of all.

Later that evening, after her relatives had left for their own apartments, Lily finally had a chance to talk about all of this with her father.

"Is something going to happen to us, Pop?" she asked as he tucked the blanket around her. Mom was still busy cleaning up the teacups from earlier in the evening. Lily and her parents shared the small room, so there was never any privacy. Still, Mom pretended not to listen, busying herself with working at the sink.

"Lily, my darling, you mustn't worry," said Pop. "I'm sorry we scared you this afternoon. The radio report was a surprise to us, that's all."

Lily gazed at her father. He was such a caring man, sometimes more of a mother than Mom. Usually, a few gentle words from Pop would be enough to drive her fears away. But this time she would not be quieted. "Willi said that the Japanese soldiers are going to get us now."

Pop interrupted. "I told you, Lily, there's nothing to worry about."

Still Lily persisted. "But Willi said that the Japanese army is as bad as the Nazis. Is that true?"

Her father's mouth stiffened into a tight line. "I'm going to have to have a word with your Uncle Willi. That's it with all of the ghost stories." He leaned close to Lily and held her in his gaze. "Now you listen to me. Nothing is going to happen to you, or to us, do you understand?"

Lily nodded, not trusting herself to speak. Mom had stopped drying the dishes and was frozen now, watching the exchange.

"Good! Now let's read. What shall it be tonight? A fairy tale?" Without waiting for an answer, Pop reached for the book next to Lily's bed and opened it to one of the pages. The book was a favorite of Lily's, one of the ones that she had brought with her from Vienna. It was filled with stories that she loved, such as *Snow White and Rose Red*, *Trusty John*, and *The Shoemaker and the Elves*. Tonight it was going to be the story of *The Wolf and the Seven Kids*.

"A mother goat left her seven kids to go and find food," Pop began, as Lily settled back onto her pillow. Pop's voice rose and fell as he read. In the story, the mother goat warned her little ones to be on guard for the wolf who was known to prowl in the woods. Before long, the wolf arrived in disguise, asking to be let in. At first, the little ones refused, mindful of their mother's warning. But after the wolf had returned several times, they finally let him in. He ate all of the kids, except for the youngest, who hid in the cupboard. When the mother returned, she was anguished to see that six of her children were gone. She and the remaining little goat went to look for the wolf and found him sleeping by the river. The mother goat cut open the stomach of the wolf to retrieve her babies who were happily still alive. In their place she placed heavy rocks and sewed the wolf up. When he awakened, he went to the river to drink, but the weight of the rocks in his stomach pushed him into the river and he drowned.

"So the mother goat and her seven little kids were happily reunited and lived together in safety from then on," Pop concluded, shutting the book with a soft thud.

"It's such a sad story," Lily said, even though she had heard it many times before. "The wolf was horrible, and those poor babies!"

"But the ending is a happy one," her father reminded her, kissing her lightly on the forehead. "All the children were saved, and that monster of a wolf was killed. The family was together once more."

Lily pulled the blanket up to her chin and rolled over to face the wall, treasuring those last words. Her family was together as well. And they were safe – at least for the time being.

Chapter 3

December 8, 1941

Lily left for school early the next morning, flying out the door of the apartment along with her best friend, Susie Stern. The truth is, Susie was much more than a friend; she was what Lily called her "almost cousin." Susie and her family had also escaped from Vienna at the same time as Lily. In fact, both Susie's and Lily's families sailed on the same ship. What's more, Susie was Uncle Walter's niece; Walter and Susie's father were brothers. The two girls had known each other since they were babies. And even though Susie had lots of cousins on her side of the family, she had agreed that she and Lily could become "almost cousins" – like blood relatives, but even better.

"Good-bye, Mrs. Kinecky," Lily called to the lady who lived up the stairs. Mrs. Kinecky lived with her husband, and although they had no children, they were hardly alone. They had four big dogs that ran up and down the stairs of the building all day and night. Behind the thin walls of their apartment, Lily was often awakened by the rough scraping of dogs' nails on wooden stairs and loud, husky barking.

Lily smiled at the Chinese lady who lived next door. There were lots of children in this family, though Lily didn't talk or play with them very much. The Chinese and Jewish families usually kept to themselves; just a smile and a nod most days. Sometimes Lily longed to approach the young Chinese girls and boys who lived in her building. Her parents never stopped reminding her that unlike most other countries, it was China that had allowed the Jews of Europe to enter. It would have been nice to thank these people for the kindness that their country had shown to Jewish families. Besides, as an only child, Lily was eager to have more friends. Susie was great, but Susie also had her own siblings – two brothers. Even though they were both older, they were still company for her. But the difference in language and customs made it difficult for Lily to speak to the Chinese children. A shy wave was all she could usually manage.

"Did you hear all that news yesterday?" Lily asked, as she and Susie headed down the street toward the river. She hugged her jacket around her body and lifted the collar to cover her ears.

"Hear it? My parents wouldn't stop talking about it all night long!" Susie was a year younger than Lily, though no one could have guessed, since she stood a half a head taller. Mind you, Lily was usually the shortest one wherever she went. Everyone towered above her, from her aunts and uncles, to the other children in her class. She hated being short; she had always wanted to be tall and willowy. Lily tried to make up for her lack of height in other ways. Pop sometimes joked with her and said, "I guess you have to speak louder so everyone will hear you from down there."

"Willi says there's going to be trouble for us, here in Shanghai," Lily continued. "He says the Japanese army is going to start coming after us, just like the Nazis did back in Vienna."

At this Susie looked thoughtful. "I don't know," she replied after a long pause. "I think the Japanese police are way too busy watching the Chinese people in this city. I don't think they're going to pay much attention to us."

It was true that the Chinese citizens of Shanghai suffered under their Japanese conquerors. Jobs had been taken away from the Chinese, along with their homes, leaving many with no way to support themselves and nowhere to live. The majority of Chinese families ended up in an area of Shanghai called Hongkew on the other side of Suzhou Creek. Hongkew was known to be the poorest part of the city. Lily never went there.

The Chinese people of Shanghai seemed so much worse off than Lily. All around her, rickshaws rolled down the street, pulled by Chinese *coolies* who wore dark cotton pants and tunics, heavily stained with sweat and dirt. The veins on their legs bulged as they pulled their loads of passengers. On their heads they wore wide-brimmed straw hats tied tightly under their chins. Some of these coolies didn't look much older than Lily and Susie, and yet here they were, working long hours for a few cents. A man walked by the girls carrying a pole across his shoulders with a large wicker basket on either end. The baskets were filled with vegetables, so heavy that the man underneath the bowed pole was bent by the weight. Even though they had left most of their belongings behind in Vienna, Lily's family seemed to get by so much easier than the Chinese people she saw every day.

"Willi says that the Japanese are just as bad as the Nazis. And they're friends with each other!"

"Oh, Willi says this, Willi says that. You've got to stop listening to your uncle." Susie flipped her wavy hair behind her ear and pulled Lily along the street. "Look around. Do you see any Japanese soldiers? Does today look different from yesterday? Stop worrying so much, and let's get something to eat."

Susie maneuvered Lily over to a street vendor who was selling dumplings from a bamboo steamer right in the middle of the sidewalk. Most of Lily's relatives and friends would not touch this street food, fearful that the conditions for preparing it were unhealthy. The vendor picked up two steaming dumplings with a pair of chopsticks, placed them on a square of brown paper, and handed them to the girls.

"*Xie, xie,*" said Lily. In the three years that she had lived in

Shanghai, she had not learned much more Chinese than this simple thank-you.

The vendor smiled. Then he blew his nose between his fingers and flung the gooey mass behind him, wiping his hands across his chest when he was finished. Lily didn't even flinch. Would she get sick from the food? She never seemed to care about that, and neither did Susie. The girls wasted no time biting into their treats. The casing was soft and slightly chewy and the unidentified meat inside steamed after the first bite.

Late now, the girls picked up the pace and made their way quickly toward the Bund, the main boardwalk that encircled the river and ran the length of Shanghai. They walked by streets with American-sounding names, like Broadway, streets that had at one time been hard to pronounce, like *Chaoufoong*, and streets that sounded like they were in a fairy tale, like Bubbling Well. Both Lily and Susie lived in an area of the city known as the French Concession. Most people simply called it Frenchtown. Along with Jews, Frenchtown was inhabited by British, French, and Americans. Many of them lived and worked along the Bund, a tree-lined boulevard, with apartment buildings, hotels, cafés, shops, and theaters. Pop sometimes called it Little Vienna, because it reminded him so much of their home. From the Bund you could look out onto the harbor and see ships with flags from many nations. In between these larger anchored vessels were dozens of Chinese *junks*, flat bamboo boats with billowing sails. It was at the port along the

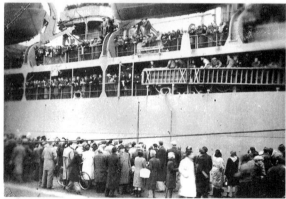

To reach Shanghai, Lily and her family sailed on board the *Conte Biancamano.*

Bund that Lily and Susie had arrived from Vienna aboard a ship called the *Conte Biancamano*, catching their first sight of the city that seemed to go on forever. Shanghai had seemed so dirty back then, nothing like the unspoiled cleanliness of Vienna. But in the three years since arriving here, Lily's impression of Shanghai had changed. Everything was comfortable now. Shanghai had become her home, perhaps even more so than the Vienna she had left behind. Mom said that it was amazing how you got used to what you lived with, so that in time, something that was once strange became familiar.

Lily was thinking about school and what reason she could give her teacher for being late that morning. Lily attended the École Municipale Française Rémi, a French-language Catholic school. The *directeur* was strict and would not be easily fooled by excuses. But Lily was a decent student, especially in French, English, and Arithmetic. M. De Chollet often wrote *Bien* or even *Très bien* on her report card next to these subjects. Perhaps Lily's tardiness would be forgiven without too much trouble.

"Where is everyone?" Lily asked. Things suddenly seemed much quieter than usual. On a normal day it was so much harder for the girls to make their way through the thick mass of people that filled the streets from early in the day until late at night. "Do you think it's because of the news on the radio?"

"I was just wondering the same thing," Susie replied. "Even the bicycles have disappeared." Their bells normally kept up a steady tune that clashed with the sounds of car horns and screeching tires.

Something was definitely peculiar and just a bit eerie. Lily was deep in thought as she and Susie rounded a corner onto the Bund. She was so focussed on thinking about the near-empty streets that she was surprised by a massive crowd gathered close to the main road. It seemed as if the entire population of Shanghai was there, pushing and shoving to get closer to something that was happening on the Bund. But what?

"So this is where everyone is. Do you have any idea what's going

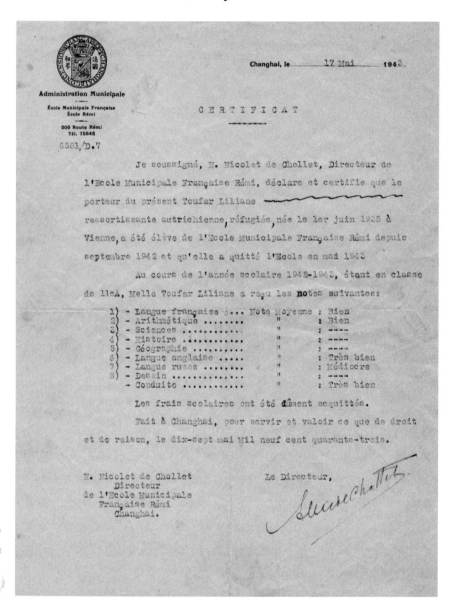

Lily received her best grades in English when she was
a student at the École Municipale Française Rémi.

on?" Susie asked as a group of Chinese children elbowed past the girls, trying to squeeze their way in front of the taller grown-ups.

"I think we should find out," Lily replied, grabbing her friend's hand.

Susie resisted. "I don't know. Maybe we shouldn't be here."

Lily would have none of that. "Don't be a chicken," she said, smiling and tugging on Susie's hand. "I want to know what's happening." With that, Lily took a deep breath and plunged into the throng of people, tightening her grip on Susie; she did not want to lose her friend in this mob. Nearly suffocating in the swarm, the girls pushed and nudged and maneuvered their way inch by inch until, with one last shove, they found themselves at the front of the crowd. The smile evaporated from Lily's face at the sight that greeted them.

The Japanese army was out in full force parading down the Bund. They were there to celebrate their victory in attacking the United States. And they were there to show how powerful they were. First came the tanks, massive and intimidating, barrelling down the boulevard. Hundreds of Japanese soldiers followed, marching in straight lines, eyes forward. In perfect formation, they thrust one leg stiffly out in front of the other, slamming it hard onto the pavement with a loud bang. The sound that filled the air was like a slow deep drumbeat that vibrated up Lily's legs and into the pit of her stomach. The soldiers wore helmets and carried rifles up against their shoulders, with bayonets fixed and ready. Their faces showed no expression. Lily could see that many of them were still young boys. Their cheeks were pale and smooth, without the slightest sign of a beard.

What was more disturbing than the soldiers who marched by, were the Chinese people who lined the road to watch. There were no cheers around Lily and Susie, no shouts of joy or excitement. The citizens of Shanghai held their heads low upon their chests. They were there to witness this parade of power, but not to celebrate it.

The two girls watched with all of the other people, unable to say a word. In the distance, the bells from Big Ben, the Customs House clock tower, began to chime out the hour. Lily silently counted the beats – *seven, eight, nine.* It was only after the parade had passed, and all that was left was an echo of the drumming of soldiers' boots, that Susie finally turned to Lily.

"Your Uncle Willi may be right," she said in a whisper. "I think there's going to be trouble."

Chapter 4

December 9, 1941

The radio was crackling again as Lily rose for school the next morning.

I ask that the Congress declare that since the unprovoked and dastardly attack by Japan on Sunday, December 7th, 1941, a state of war has existed between the United States and the Japanese Empire.[1]

It was President Roosevelt of the United States, speaking about war between his country and Japan. His voice was deep and somber. Lily dressed quickly and joined her parents for breakfast at the small table. Pop sipped his tea and glanced at his daughter, smiling faintly. "Did you sleep well, Lily?"

She nodded, staring down at the plate of porridge Mom had placed in front of her and trying to keep her eyes open. The truth was, Lily had not slept much the previous night. Every time she closed her eyes, all she could see were the Japanese soldiers marching down the Bund, pounding their boots into the pavement and raising their guns up into the air. She had not told her parents about seeing the parade. They looked worried enough about the news that was unfolding around the world. They would not have been happy to know that their young daughter had pushed her way to the front of a military procession. *Better to keep that information to myself,* Lily thought.

"What does it all mean, Pop?" she asked, nodding toward the radio.

"There were a lot of Americans killed in the Japanese attack on Hawaii yesterday," Pop said, rubbing his eyes and shaking his head. "No one expected the Japanese to be that powerful. After what happened, America can't stand by. That's why President Roosevelt has declared war on Japan. We knew it was coming," he added, looking up at his wife.

But what does it mean for us? That's the question that Lily really wanted to ask. She leaned toward her father.

"Pop," she began, choosing her words carefully. "If the Japanese army is getting stronger, do you think they will try to do anything here in Shanghai?"

"Are you still thinking about all those stories your Uncle Willi was telling you?" Mom stood above Lily, hands on her hips. "Is that what's bothering you this morning?" Mom could always tell when something was up with Lily.

How do I ask this without talking about the parade? Lily took a deep breath. "I'm just wondering…" she began. "Let's say more Japanese soldiers came here. Do you think they'd do anything to us?"

"That's enough talking," Mom said, removing Lily's plate. "Between the radio broadcasts and Willi's stories, it's enough for all of us. It's time for you to go to school, Lily."

Lily sighed. She put on her coat and hat, and picked up her bag of books, pausing to hug her father before she left. "Will you read to me tonight?" she asked.

Pop reached up to pinch Lily's cheek. "Your turn to choose the book."

Lily had only one wish as she headed out the door and that was for no more bad news in the world. But that was not to be. On December 11, the radio sputtered out the news that Germany and Italy had declared war on the United States. The U.S. shot back with a quick counter-declaration of war on Germany and Italy. The world was on the brink of a battle that was bigger than any Lily could have imagined. Mom and Pop still resisted answering her questions. And Willi was the worst, teasing his niece more than he usually did with half-truths and warnings about the Japanese army coming to get her. She would cover her ears and finally push him away, running for the safety of her small bed. After what Lily had witnessed on the Bund, she was starting to believe whatever Willi said! Pop had to step in again and tell him to stop tormenting her.

Several weeks later, Lily and her parents were invited for Christmas dinner at the Missionary Home. Although her family didn't celebrate this holiday, the invitation was a great excuse to try to put worries aside and dress up for a fancy evening. Besides, the food that the missionaries served was always delicious, and there was lots of it.

The mission was run by Mother Lawler and her daughter, Beatrice. They and most of the other missionaries were Americans, stationed in Shanghai where they had taken on the challenge of trying to convert the locals to Christianity. Mother Lawler had been the first person whom Lily and her parents had met when they stepped off the ship and onto the shore of Shanghai back in 1938. Lily recalled how overwhelmed they had all been by the sights and sounds of the port, along with the smells and the crush of thousands of desperate and confused people. And then they had heard the voice of Mother Lawler.

"Welcome," she had said, reaching her arms wide to hug Lily. Mother Lawler had piercing blue eyes and gray hair that was tied in a tight bun at the back of her head. Lily yielded to the embrace, even though she had no idea who this woman was. "I'm here to help you," Mother Lawler had added. "First things first. If you'll come with me,

I have a place where you can stay. It's temporary, but so much better than the alternative."

The alternative that Mother Lawler had referred to was the *heims,* a series of barrack-like buildings, constructed to house Jewish refugees upon their arrival in Shanghai. In fact, "heim" was a German word that meant home, though these places could hardly be called by that name. The conditions there were horrible! Lily had once visited a heim where Susie's friend, Jacob, lived. Jacob and hundreds of other refugees were crowded together in one room. Families were separated from one another by torn sheets that hung on rods suspended from wooden beams. These makeshift curtains offered next to no privacy. Food in the heims was inedible, and toilets were non-existent; people had to use buckets that were set into badly constructed wooden shacks. "I don't know if I would have survived in such a place, not even for one night," Mom often said.

By contrast, the Missionary Home had offered Lily and her family a private room, clean sheets on their beds, and food that was nourishing and plentiful. They knew that, in exchange, they would have to live with Mother Lawler's determined goal to convert them. But it was worth it. They had stayed for several months until Pop had found the small apartment where they now lived.

Now, Mother Lawler was at the door of the mission to greet Lily's family. "Merry Christmas to all of you!" she exclaimed. "We're here to celebrate the birth of our savior, and to give thanks to God for all that we have, even in these difficult times." Lily allowed herself to be hugged, as she always did. Mother Lawler was kind, and her daughter, Beatrice, was warm and bubbly. But still, Lily was always uneasy around the missionaries. She didn't like all this talk of God and Christianity. While she respected the missionaries' views, she didn't believe in Jesus and never would. Didn't Mother Lawler know that she was Jewish? It's true that Lily's family did not follow all the rules and customs of their religion. Back in Vienna, they had not attended synagogue except on the high holy days. But still, they would never have abandoned their religion, no matter how caring the missionaries were.

Lily and her parents entered the elegant dining room and sat at the long table with the other families whom Mother Lawler had invited. Susie was there, and she and Lily quickly shifted around so that they were seated next to each other. The table was laden with beautiful china dishes and rows of silver cutlery. Lily had no idea which fork to start with and which spoon to use. Susie seemed to know what to do, so Lily watched carefully and followed her lead.

Before beginning the meal, Mother Lawler passed a jar filled with small strips of paper around the table. "There is a psalm written on every piece of paper," Mother Lawler said. "Each one of you must pull one out and read it aloud before passing the jar on."

Most of the guests murmured their approval, diving into the jar as if they were reaching for a prize, and reciting their prayer with enthusiasm. When it was Lily's turn, she pulled a strip from the jar and read in a clear voice, "A banquet is prepared with my cup running over. My head is anointed with oil…" Mother Lawler looked on, smiling broadly. Lily ducked her head and began to dip into the soup that was placed in front of her, a light fishy broth filled with bits of vegetables.

The conversation at the table immediately turned to talk of war, and Lily paused between spoonfuls of soup to hear every word. She had been trying to learn the truth about what was happening in the world from the conversations she overhead her parents whisper late into the night when they thought she was fast asleep. But it was hard to figure out how all this would affect the Jews of Shanghai. Even though her aunts and uncles were always there, listening to the radio and trying to hear bits and pieces of world news, the radio was turned off when Lily asked too many questions. Then the conversation would come to an abrupt end, or voices would lower to a whisper. Aunt Stella or Uncle Walter would jump up and quickly move the radio back into its spot on a corner table. But even then, they would look longingly in its direction, wondering if they were missing a crucial piece of information.

"The Japanese army is everywhere in the city," Pop was saying. "Their flags are flying from every building – that big red circle on a white background. They call it the rising sun flag. Well, there are suns rising everywhere in Shanghai." He snorted as he said this.

The news of the parade on the Bund had spread across the city, though Lily's parents still didn't know she'd been there to watch.

"British, French, and Americans are all being barred from the city, or arrested if they don't leave," added Mom. "All American and British ships have been sunk in the harbor."

Lily had also seen the smoke and flames rising from the ships anchored off the Bund. The sight of dozens of boats on fire had only added to her fears.

"Aren't you afraid for your safety, Mother Lawler?" asked Mom.

Mother Lawler shook her head. "We're here to do God's work," she said calmly. "No one is going to force us to leave."

"Maybe it's not such a bad thing to have America in this war," Pop continued. "We need someone like Roosevelt to go after Hitler."

At this, the guests around the table all murmured their agreement. One man thumped his fist on the table and exclaimed, "More than thirty-five hundred Americans were injured or killed in the attack on Pearl Harbor. Roosevelt won't stop until he's made up for every life lost."

Susie nudged Lily under the table. "Can we leave?" Lily shook her head. It infuriated her that the grown-ups did not include her in their discussions. It was hard to understand everything from the bits and pieces she was discovering. It was like knowing only the beginning and middle of a story that Pop might read at night, but never learning the ending. But when she pressed her parents to tell her the truth about what was happening in Shanghai and the world, their response was always the same.

"The family is together and that's all that's important," Pop would say.

"You mustn't worry, Lily," Mom would add. "We're fine, aren't we? And nothing is going to change that."

Lily didn't believe that anymore. At least here at Mother Lawler's, she could eavesdrop on the conversation, unnoticed. Susie nudged her again, but Lily shook her hand away. Just then, Mother Lawler glanced up. "I think it's time for the young ones to go into the main salon," she said. "This conversation is not for them and there is something special going on there that I think they will all enjoy."

Lily sighed, deprived once again of hearing the discussion.

"Finally!" Susie exclaimed as all the children excused themselves and made their way into the other room. "I didn't think we'd ever be able to get out of there. I'm not sure what's worse, the prayers and psalms that Mother Lawler makes us recite, or all that talk of war." She added that she'd had enough of both.

Lily didn't know what to say. She didn't know how to explain to her friend that not understanding the whole truth was worse for her than hearing it. Instead, she followed Susie into the main room where Mother Lawler had said that there was something special happening. When the children entered, they were greeted by the sight of the giant Christmas tree, decorated with lit candles and small ornaments. Lily had to admit, it was beautiful. As she was admiring the tree at one end of the room, there was a big commotion at the other.

"Ho, ho, ho, Merry Christmas!" bellowed a voice behind her. "Come and see what Santa Claus has brought for all of you wonderful children!"

Susie and the other boys and girls gathered around Santa, reaching their arms up to accept one of the gifts that he offered from his big bag. But not Lily.

Santa spotted her standing apart from the crowd and marched over to stand in front of her. "Well, well, little girl. And what's your name?"

Lily froze. She stared up at the round man with the red, puffy cheeks and thundering voice and her heart raced. She was terrified of Santa Claus and always had been. She remembered that her teacher, on another Christmas, had handed out pictures of him for the children to color. Lily had colored him with dark greens and blues, almost wiping out his image. The teacher had been angry when Lily had shown her the drawing.

Santa would not give up. "Cat got your tongue, little girl?" he roared.

"I...I..." Lily stammered. She didn't know why Santa scared her so much. Was it Uncle Willi and all his talk of ghosts and evil creatures? Is that why this giant red-suited man seemed so terrifying?

"Come look into Santa's big bag and see if there's something you'd like."

That was enough to send Lily running for the dining room. She was just in time to catch the end of the grown-up conversation. And it stopped her in her tracks. Pop was speaking once more.

"Hitler is trying to make all of Europe *Judenfrei* – free of Jews. Will he convince the Japanese Imperial Army to do the same here in Shanghai?"

The other gentleman who had spoken earlier nodded and thumped the table once more. "Japan will not want to do anything to anger Hitler."

"How is it possible that the war in Europe is following us here?" Mom asked, shaking her head in disbelief. "Haven't we all had enough trouble in our lives?"

At that moment, Mom caught sight of Lily standing in the doorway. She nudged her husband and pointed at their daughter. Pop cleared his throat and took a deep breath. "Let's not jump to conclusions," he said quickly. "The troubles in the rest of the world are still so far away. Things may settle down sooner than we think."

Lily wasn't so sure.

Chapter 5

February, 1942

As Christmas and New Year passed, the Japanese presence in Shanghai continued to grow. Troops patrolled on every corner now, not just on the Bund. Every day, while on their way to school, Lily and Susie passed by soldiers who, like vultures, eyed the citizens of Shanghai. Lily always kept her head down and clutched her bag of books to her chest, hoping the soldiers wouldn't notice her. Susie did the same. The two girls were never stopped. But others were not as lucky. And those who were detained most often were the Chinese citizens.

One day, Lily watched as a Japanese soldier pulled an elderly Chinese man off a bicycle and ordered him to open the big cloth bundle he carried on his back. The old man crouched down and cradled his head in his arms. He was crying and muttering something.

And though Lily could not understand a word he was saying, she could only imagine that he was begging the soldier to leave him alone, and to let him go home to his family. The soldier just laughed and grabbed some melons and heads of lettuce from the old man's pack before ordering him to his feet and kicking him on his way.

Lily felt so sad to see elderly Chinese men and women bow to the gruff Japanese soldiers who barked orders at them and forced them to open their packages. She longed to help. She wanted to cry out to the soldiers and say, "Stop hurting those people. They aren't doing anything to you!" And yet she knew that there was nothing she could do, just as the Chinese citizens had no choice but to submit to these inspections.

"It seems so much worse for everyone than it was before Pearl Harbor," Lily said to Susie one day after witnessing a soldier grab a bicycle from a young Chinese girl. The girl stood sobbing in the middle of the road, while all around her, people hurried by, barely acknowledging her troubles.

"We're lucky they're not coming after Jews," Susie replied.

That was exactly what was worrying Lily. "Why are you saying that?" she demanded.

"My father said that the Japanese soldiers are determined to show that they are in command of everyone here in Shanghai. But as long as the army is focused on the Chinese people, they won't bother much with us."

Lily and her family first lived in the French Concession,
an area of Shanghai that everyone simply called Frenchtown.

Is that it? Lily wondered. Had the Chinese citizens become some kind of protective barrier, standing in front of the Jews of Shanghai, and taking all the abuse? That made their predicament so much more confusing for Lily. While it was painful to see these men, women, and children treated so badly, Lily was relieved that the Japanese army was targeting them and not Jewish families. Yet, she still worried about what would happen if and when the Japanese army got tired of bullying the Chinese. Would the Jews be next?

Lily's parents, like everyone else, were also on edge and avoiding all of her questions. Pop had even stopped reading stories to Lily at night. "Perhaps you could read on your own, my darling," he would say. "I'm just a little tired." Lily had no choice but to retreat to her bed with her books. These days, she lived in her head, wondering and worrying about what would happen. Each day that she came home safely was a day that she gave silent thanks that she and the other Jewish residents of Shanghai were not under attack. No one was banging down their door to come and get them. No Jews were being arrested the way they had been on the eve of her family's escape from Vienna. As the early days of 1942 marched on, Lily continued to hope that the war against Jews in Europe would stay there and not come to the shores of Shanghai.

Lily arrived home from school in early February to an empty apartment. She shivered as she walked through the door, not bothering to remove her jacket. Sometimes it felt as if it was just as cold inside as it was outside. Her parents were at work. Pop did odd jobs around Frenchtown. Sometimes he peddled clothing and other wares. Sometimes he made and sold shoes from scraps of leather that he obtained by bartering. Sometimes he helped Stella and Walter in their coffee house. He even did manicures and pedicures for some of the Jewish men and women in their neighborhood. He joked that he could make the foulest feet look as delicate as porcelain. He left their home before seven in the morning, often returning after nine at night.

Mom worked equally long hours at a convent where she taught embroidery and needlework to young Chinese girls. Mom's embroidery was intricate, like works of art stitched into fabric. She had owned a needlepoint store in Vienna years earlier where several people worked for her. Her treadle sewing machine proved to be one of the most important items that the family had managed to bring to Shanghai. It had traveled along with them by train to Italy, on the ship here to the port, and from the Missionary Home to this apartment. It now sat in a corner, piled with the embroidery and needlepoint that was ready to be sewn into handbags and other items. When they had first arrived in Shanghai, Lily used to go with her mother to the convent. There were rabbits kept in small cages in the back, and Lily would help feed them. That had stopped once she started going to school.

After that, Lily was sometimes left on her own at the end of the day. Occasionally, Aunt Nini looked after her while Mom worked late. But more often than not, it was Oma who was there when Lily returned home from school. Oma always had a small snack waiting, and Lily would sit at the table in the center of the room and lead her grandmother through the things that had happened at school that day. Oma's English had not been very good and that was the only language that Lily wanted to speak. Lily would patiently explain the lessons she had learned and the homework she had to complete.

"*Gott in himmel!*" Oma would exclaim in her native German. "God in heaven, go slower, Lily. I can't understand when you speak so fast."

Lily's Oma.

Lily would repeat the stories, slower now, carefully pronouncing every word so that her grandmother could follow. Lily's heart always ached when she thought of Oma. She missed their little private conversations. Their relationship had not always been smooth. Lily remembered that she had sometimes tormented her grandmother, and one time in particular stood out in her memory.

In addition to hating her height, Lily also hated her reddish hair and the freckles that filled the bridge of her nose and spilled onto her round cheeks and forehead. Round faces ran on Mom's side of the family; she had inherited the freckles from her Pop. Well, there was not much that she could do about her freckles or her height. She was stuck with being the shortest in her family. But she figured that there was something she could do about her hair.

One day, about a year after her family had arrived in Shanghai, Lily came home from school and decided that she would dye her hair another color. Anything would be better than the mousy reddish blonde she had. No one was home that day, so Lily rummaged through the apartment and finally found a bottle of black ink that

Oma riding a rickshaw in Shanghai.

Mom used to write notes. Lily inspected the bottle, opening it carefully and sniffing the contents. The smell was nasty, but it would surely do the trick.

She walked out onto the balcony holding the bottle of dye. *No one will know a thing*, she thought, *especially if I don't make a mess inside*. Not once did she imagine what her parents were going to think of the results. She lowered her head and began to pour the contents of the bottle onto her hair. Drops of black liquid began to mass on the wooden slats under her feet. *Oh no*, Lily thought, suddenly realizing that her plan might not have been the smartest. But it was too late to stop. Just as she was pouring the last drops onto her scalp, she heard the apartment door open and Oma step inside.

"*Was haben Sie gemacht?* What have you done?" Oma cried as soon as she saw the mess on Lily's head and on the balcony floor.

Oma had been furious, chasing Lily around the apartment, her hand high in the air, ready to swat her grandchild if she caught her. Lily dodged this way and that, avoiding Oma's outstretched hand. Lily may have been small, but she was fast. She doubted that her grandmother would actually hit her; that had never happened before. But she was not going to take any chances. Just as Lily was about to run out the door of the apartment, there was a loud thud behind her. When she looked back, she saw her grandmother stretched out on the floor, not moving. Oma had fallen, tripping over a small stool that Lily often sat on. The dyed hair, along with the possibility of punishment, was instantly forgotten as Lily rushed to her grandmother's side and helped her up and into a chair. It wasn't clear who was moaning louder, Oma, who was obviously in pain from her fall, or Lily, who was in anguish and crying over the entire incident.

After that day, everything seemed to go downhill for Oma — at least, that's what Lily believed. Oma became weaker. She stopped playing the piano in Stella and Walter's coffee house. She had difficulty climbing the stairs, and she fell into a deep sadness that would not lift.

"I'm so sorry," Lily would whisper as she knelt beside Oma's bed, longing for her grandmother to talk to her, or even yell at her. "Open your eyes, Oma. Please! I can tell you about my day at school. I'll talk slowly so that you understand every word." Lily was met with silence.

"This is not your fault," Mom told Lily every day after that and even after Oma died and was buried in the Jewish cemetery on the outskirts of Shanghai. "Your grandmother was sick, probably before we ever came to this city."

"If she hadn't been chasing me, this would never have happened," Lily replied sadly.

Mom sighed and shook her head. "It was only a matter of time before she died. This had nothing to do with you."

Lily wanted to believe that, but couldn't. It took months after the incident with the shoe dye for Lily's hair to return to its normal color. It took much longer to recover from Oma's death. Lily thought of that now as she rummaged through the small icebox, looking for something to fill the hollow feeling in her stomach. There was nothing there, just some smelly cheese that Pop liked. Lily wandered out into the hallway, wondering if Mom would be home soon, and if she would bring a treat for her – maybe a little sugary bun from the convent dining room, or some steamed vegetables wrapped in rice paper.

Mrs. Kinecky's dogs nearly pushed Lily over as she walked out into the stairwell. Two of them were almost as big as she was. She stepped quickly out of their way before she could be trampled, and found herself next to the open door of the apartment belonging to their Chinese neighbors. Lily peered inside, curious about who was home and what they might be doing. The mother was busy cooking dinner in front of the stove. Well, it wasn't actually a stove. It was just a large clay flowerpot with a metal grid inside to hold the burning coals. Most families had these cooking stoves. It had been a disaster the first time that Mom had tried to light the coals in her own flowerpot, Lily recalled. Match after precious match had been discarded while Lily tried to fan the coals for a spark and Mom frantically tried to add bits of paper to create a fire. It had taken a long time to figure out how to do it properly. The Chinese woman next door was an expert. The coals were red hot and a pot of water had been placed on top to boil. A small child clung to her mother's leg, sucking on two of her fingers. She looked up at Lily in the doorway and then quickly lowered her eyes. The heavy smell of garlic and ginger filled the small room and wafted out into the hallway where Lily stood watching. The mother approached the pot once more, this time carrying a live lobster. It squirmed and arched in her hands as she lowered it gently into the boiling water. Just as the wriggling lobster hit the bubbling water, it began to squeal and scream. It was a sound that Lily had never heard before. She had no idea that it was just the sound of steam escaping from the shell. In her mind, the lobster was screaming in pain. The cries were so unbearable that Lily began to yell and scream as well.

"Stop, stop, you're hurting it!" Lily cried. She was frozen on the spot, eyes fixed on the pot of boiling water and the lobster still squirming inside.

The startled woman looked up and rushed to Lily's side. "No hurt, no hurt," she said, stroking Lily's arm and trying to quiet her. Her young child was wrapped around her leg now, as if she feared that she might be next into the pot!

Lily saw and heard nothing except the ongoing screams from the boiling water. Seconds later, she found her legs and turned and fled to the safety of her apartment, slamming the door behind her. When Mom arrived home some time later, Lily was still curled in a ball on her bed, reliving the horror of having witnessed the death of the lobster. Mom had to coax the story out of her, trying not to laugh as her daughter described the scene.

It took a long time for Lily to calm down, and even late into the night, she could still picture the lobster writhing and squealing. Perhaps she was so distraught about the lobster because of her earlier memories of Oma howling in pain after falling in the apartment. Whatever the reason, one thing was for sure. The lobster incident had wiped out every thought she'd had of the war in Europe or the possibility of it arriving on the shores of Shanghai. Perhaps that was one good thing that had come of the whole episode. "I will never eat lobster as long as I live," Lily whispered into the darkness. And with that, she rolled over and went to sleep.

Chapter 6

May, 1942

Several months passed, and on a warm spring Sunday in May, Mom was hunched over at the table, writing something on sheets of paper spread out in front of her. Mom was the one who was in charge of the finances. Each month, she carefully recorded every cent that was earned and spent, making sure the family would have enough to live on. "Thank goodness for your mother's business sense," Pop always said. "If it were up to me, we'd probably be out on the streets!" Lily knew that her mother was not like some other moms who cooked and cleaned all day. The sound of Mom's pen scratching over the paper was a soft background accompaniment for Lily as she lay reading on her bed. But today, Mom's pen had gone quiet. It was the silence that made Lily look up from her book.

The door to the balcony was wide open and sunshine poured into the small apartment. Lily could see that Mom had pulled some old letters from a small box she kept under her bed. She was pouring over the letters and muttering under her breath. Occasionally, she dabbed at her eyes with a hanky that she kept in the sleeve of her blouse. Lily had seen her mother read these letters before and was just about to say something when Pop spoke first.

"This does you no good, Erna," he said, shaking his head. Pop was stacking rolls of textiles and fabrics into a big pile. "I've told you to stop reading the letters from home."

Mom waved an envelope in the air. It was pale blue and thin as a layer of skin. It fluttered in the warm breeze that drifted in from outside. "I'm relieved that our family managed to get out of Vienna safely. But there are friends we left behind. I haven't heard from Berta or Simon in months, not since they were moved out of their home. And no news from Dora in over a year."

"I'm just as worried as you are," Pop said. "But you won't get any answers, no matter how many times you re-read those letters."

Mom opened her mouth to reply and then clamped it shut.

Lily said nothing. Her book lay beside her, open but forgotten as she listened closely to what her parents were saying. She knew that in the years since they had arrived in Shanghai, Jews back home had been moved into areas of cities and towns that were just like prisons. And not just in Austria; it was happening in Germany, Czechoslovakia,

Poland, and other countries. These places were called ghettos, and from what her parents had told her, the conditions there were inhumane. But when Lily pressed her mother for news of what had happened to the friends they left behind, Mom would shake her head and refuse to answer. Willi was the one who said they were probably all dead.

"Here! Just listen to what Berta wrote." Mom began to read from one of the letters.

> *...They took my jewelry and the last of our money – just came and stole our things while we were forced to stand there and watch. But now we've been told that we are being relocated to a new town. Perhaps there will be more for us there. It certainly can't be any worse than it's been here...*

Mom looked up. "Relocated! What does that mean?"

Pop shook his head and sighed heavily.

Mom persisted. "Where have they been sent? And why have we heard nothing?"

"Susie's family hasn't heard from their relatives, either."

At the sound of Lily's voice, Mom and Pop turned around as if they suddenly realized that Lily was in the room and listening in on their conversation. Mom rose from the sewing machine and shoved her letters back into the box.

Pop cleared his throat. "I'm going into Hongkew today. I've got to deliver these materials to a store there. Lily, would you like to come with me?"

Lily wanted to say more – ask some questions about the ghettos and what it meant to live there – but it seemed her chance was gone.

Pop continued. "I thought you could keep me company."

Pop's eyes looked tired. It was something that Lily had noticed ever since all that bad news had started arriving about the war in Europe and America. In fact, Lily realized that Pop hadn't told a joke or even laughed in weeks. She missed that. This was a chance to spend a morning with him, just the two of them. That was something else Lily had missed in the previous weeks. But Hongkew! That was the place where the poorest Chinese families lived. Lily had never set foot in that part of Shanghai. She was not sure she wanted to.

"Is it safe, Fritz?" Mom had pushed her box of letters back underneath her bed. "I mean for the child."

"She'll be with me," Pop replied. "No harm will come to her." He turned once again to his daughter. "So what will it be, Lily? Do you want to come on an outing with your Pop?"

Lily rose from her bed. "Let's go," she said.

She grabbed her sweater, but not before Mom had stuffed the pockets with two apples and two biscuits. "In case you get hungry," she said. "Now, keep hold of your father's hand," Mom instructed, "and make sure you listen to him. No running off. Lily, do you hear me?"

Mom's voice followed Lily out the door and down the stairs.

She turned to wave at Mom and then placed her hand firmly in her father's grasp, walking quickly as she tried to keep up with his long stride. The sun shone brightly on Frenchtown and within minutes, Lily had worked up a sweat and unbuttoned her sweater. Even Pop's forehead glistened in the warmth of the spring day. It felt as if everyone had come out onto the streets. Rickshaws moved by at a brisk pace. Bicycles swerved around and in between cars and pedestrians. Street peddlers sang out to the passers-by, urging them to stop and sample their wares. The Japanese police were out as well, standing on street corners with their guns by their sides. But it seemed as if the warm weather had softened them as well. No one was being stopped. Lily felt calm. Today there would be no radios with news of the war and no scary predictions, no more talk of ghettos or what had happened to relatives left behind, and no Japanese soldiers coming after them. Today was a day for spending time with her father.

"Shall we play a game?" Pop asked. "Perhaps a game of I Spy?"

Lily practically squealed with delight. "You start!" she shouted.

Pop paused and glanced behind him. "I spy, here on the street, something that is brown."

Lily looked around and up and down the busy road they were on. Then she said. "Is it the brown dog walking right behind us?"

Pop nodded.

"That was too easy," said Lily. Pop had given it away as soon as he looked behind him.

Her father laughed. "Next time, I'll think of something more challenging."

It was Lily's turn. She paused, turning her head to the left and the right, and then she said. "I spy, here on the street, something that is red."

"Is it the red on that wagon over there?" Lily shook her head. Pop pointed to a street vendor. "What about the red from the radishes in that man's basket?" That wasn't it either. Pop made three more guesses and then shrugged his shoulders. "I give up," he said.

Lily laughed. "It's the red in the sweater I'm wearing." Pop had missed the most obvious thing of all. Lily was so involved in her game that, at first, she didn't even realize that everything around her was changing dramatically. She and her father were leaving Frenchtown far behind them and were approaching the district of Hongkew. Houses and apartments were smaller, pressed close to one another, swallowing the light until all that was left was a dark, dirty haze. Alleyways sprouted from the main road like tentacles on an octopus. Lily grew quiet, and as she began to look around, her eyes widened at the unfamiliar sights and sounds. It felt as if they were walking into a dark and mysterious maze.

Here the streets were completely clogged as thousands of Chinese people went about their business. Within seconds, Lily and her father were surrounded by several ragged-looking children, stretching their open palms up toward Lily and Pop's faces. Pop reached into his pocket, pulled out a few cents, and handed them to the children who took off without a backward glance. A beggar hobbled by on crutches; the sores on his arms and face oozed with a yellow liquid. There were old women crouched in the entranceways of dank, crumbling buildings. Here and there, bodies were strewn across the sidewalks, while people simply stepped over them and kept on walking. Lily couldn't tell if they were dead, or just sleeping by the side of the road. She watched as a little girl squatted in a gutter to relieve herself. When the child stood up, Lily saw that her pants were slit open across the back. Lily pressed her hand up to her face and covered her mouth and nose,

The streets and alleyways in Hongkew were
dark and dirty. This one was off East Yuhang Road.

trying to keep out the overpowering smell of food mixed with urine. Smoke from dozens of street-side cooking pots filled the air and Lily's lungs. She coughed and struggled to catch her breath as she tightened her grip on her father's hand. Pop looked down at her.

"It's okay," he said. "Don't be afraid."

Lily opened her mouth to talk and then clamped it shut. She wasn't scared, she wanted to say. She just couldn't believe what she was seeing. This place was worlds away from Frenchtown, and yet it was just over the Garden Bridge and a few short miles from where she and her family had been living. *How can these two places be so close to one another and yet be so completely different? And how can people live here?*

Pop seemed to know where he was going. He maneuvered his daughter this way and that, up and down small alleys and across busy, crowded streets until they came to a small lane. At the end of that lane, Pop paused and knocked loudly on a big wooden door. Lily could hear footsteps on the other side, and then the door opened.

"Ah, Herr Toufar! Please come in." A round, short woman stood at the entranceway of a dark room. Her hair was pulled up into a big round bun that sat on the top of her head like a melon. She spread her arms wide, pulled the door back, and motioned for Lily and her father to enter. "I see you've brought your daughter with you, this time. Welcome," the woman exclaimed.

"Lily, this is Mrs. Goldstein. She has a dress shop here in Hong-kew. I've brought her some materials that she needs."

Lily said hello to the woman and entered the room behind her father. Within seconds, Pop and Mrs. Goldstein had their heads together talking about the fabrics Pop had brought. Lily looked around. Several sewing machines, just like Mom's, were lined up against the back wall. The machines hummed in unison as Chinese women, busy at work, fashioned trousers and skirts from pieces of material that they had pinned together. A couple of women glanced up at Lily, their faces expressionless, and then quickly returned to their work.

There were no windows inside the small room. The only light glowed from a bare bulb that swung from the ceiling and one small floor lamp in a corner that swayed from side to side as the women pumped the pedals of their sewing machines. Bits of dust and thread traveled up Lily's nose, and she sneezed and rubbed her eyes as they adjusted to the dim light.

It was only then that Lily noticed the Chinese boy and girl sitting together on a wooden box in another corner of the room. They were young – the boy was maybe five years old, the girl, no more than four. Their clothes were dirty and torn, and they had no shoes on their feet. Both of them had long, jet-black hair. Lily was particularly struck by the little boy. His hair was almost down to his waist and was tied in a ponytail with an elastic band. Uncle Willi had once told her that it was the custom for young Chinese boys to grow their hair long in order to protect them from the devil that came in search of little boys.

If a child's hair was long, the devil might think he was a girl and not take him away.

One of the sewing women looked up at Lily again, catching her gaze, and gesturing toward the young children. Lily understood immediately that these children were hers. *She must have brought them with her to work,* Lily thought, *just like I used to go with Mom to the convent when we first arrived in Shanghai.* Lily smiled and nodded at the woman and then smiled at the children. They lowered their eyes.

Pop was still busy with Mrs. Goldstein. Lily approached the brother and sister and bent down in front of them. The little girl grabbed her brother's arm and shrank back. *Oh, if only we could talk to each other,* Lily thought. *This would be so much easier.* She took a deep breath, extended her hand, and said, "Hello."

Seconds passed. Lily's hand remained there, suspended in the open space between her and the children. And then slowly and hesitantly, the little girl reached out to Lily. *"Ni hao,"* she replied. And the two of them shook hands.

"Lily, it's time to go."

Pop had finished his business with Mrs. Goldstein, and he stood with the door open at the entranceway of the small room. Lily reached into the pocket of her sweater and pulled out the apples and biscuits her mother had stuffed into them. She held them out to the young children. They hesitated at first, glancing back at their mother who grunted something in their direction. Then they grabbed the food and quickly began to devour it, alternating between mouthfuls of apple and bites of biscuit.

"*Xie, xie,*" they muttered, in unison. Apple juice dotted with cookie crumbs ran down their faces and onto their shirts.

Lily smiled again, stood up, and left the store with her father. At first, they were quiet on the walk back to Frenchtown. Lily was the first one to break the silence.

"That lady, Mrs. Goldstein, does she live there?"

Pop nodded. "There are some Jewish families who live in Hongkew."

"She seems very poor," Lily continued, choosing her words carefully.

"We were lucky to be able to bring some money with us from Vienna," Pop replied. "These Jewish families here have so little. This is the only living area they can afford."

"And the Chinese families?" Lily asked.

"They have even less. It's a hard life for anyone who has to live in Hongkew," Pop said.

Lily paused, thoughtfully. "It was so dirty there, Pop. And those kids looked so hungry."

"It's important for you to see this place, Lily – to know that others are not as lucky as we are."

Lily nodded. Her parents had always talked about how lucky they were to be in Shanghai, even though they'd had to give up their home in Vienna to get here. Sometimes Lily complained about how small their flat in Frenchtown was, and how cold it would become in winter. *That's nothing compared to what it must be like in Hongkew,* Lily thought. She vowed that she would try to be more grateful for the things she had. Lily grabbed her father's hand again as they crossed the Garden Bridge. It was a relief to catch sight of the Bund in the distance and to leave Hongkew far behind.

Chapter 7

February 18, 1943

It was several months after her visit to Hongkew that Lily's life changed again, in ways that she could never have imagined.

Susie was over that day, and the two girls were playing at the table in the center of the apartment. They had cut out figures from paper and glued them into empty shoeboxes Pop had given them to make little theaters. Lily painted and colored hers, and cut small holes in the sides to create windows to peer into. She had painted a woman on a stage in the box, singing to a big faceless audience. The backdrop looked just like the stage of the Eastern Theater where Lily and her father had gone to see the opera *Carmen* weeks before. Here in Shanghai, the Jewish community had created a thriving world of theater, music, and poetry. Many famous actors and actresses who also had fled Austria and Germany continued to perform on the stages of Shanghai clubs and theaters, some of them in the coffee house that Stella and Walter owned. The Jewish refugees flocked to see them.

Pop loved operas and had been excited to take Lily to see this one about a soldier who falls in love with a woman named Carmen and then loses her to a famous bullfighter. Lily, on the other hand, had not understood a word of what was being sung and did not enjoy a minute of the performance. "Besides," she had said to her father afterward, "that lady who played the part of Carmen was ugly and old!" Pop had laughed, humming the tunes they had just heard and pretending to conduct a phantom orchestra. Lily could not figure out what Pop saw in all of this. She had tried to explain it to Susie, which had led to the construction of this scene in the little shoebox.

Lily loved having Susie over to her apartment to play after school, but enjoyed visiting Susie's home even more. Susie's family was considered to be rich. Their apartment had several rooms, unlike Lily's one-room flat. There was a huge courtyard in front of Susie's building where the girls could play. Someone in the building even had a car, which was practically unheard of among the Jewish dwellers of Shanghai. But best of all, Susie's apartment had a bathtub. The only bathing facilities in Lily's building were in the hallway, in a washroom that her family shared with their neighbors. There were many hot summer days when the two girls had put on bathing suits, filled the tub in Susie's place with cool water, and sunk up to their necks, pretending they were at a swimming pool.

Lily was singing at the top of her lungs, pretending to be the opera diva from *Carmen*. Susie had her hands clamped over her ears, begging her to stop. Just then, Pop entered the apartment and sat down heavily next to the girls. *It's early for Pop to be home*, Lily thought, eager to show her father her artwork. But one look at his face was enough to bring their play to a screeching halt. Pop was white, paler than the day the radio had blared the news about the bombing of Pearl Harbor, or the night they had fled Vienna. And just like he'd done on those occasions, he pulled a handkerchief from his pocket and wiped his forehead with a trembling hand. At that moment, Mom walked into the apartment.

"Fritz, whatever is the matter?" she cried.

Pop couldn't answer. In his hands he held one of the Jewish newspapers that was published in Shanghai. He stared at the headlines for a moment, shaking his head as if he could not believe what was written, and then placed the paper down on the table in front of him. Mom, Lily, and Susie peered at it.

…Stateless refugees will be restricted to an area…in Hongkew…. All Stateless residents presently residing outside the area mentioned, shall move their business and/or residence inside the above prescribed area by May 18, 1943. Any person who violates this proclamation and interferes with its enforcement shall be liable to severe punishment….[2]

RESIDENCES, BUSINESSES OF CITY'S STATELESS REFUGEES LIMITED TO DEFINED SECTOR

'3

Measure Effective From May 18th Is Due To Military Necessity

ONLY THOSE ARRIVING SINCE 1937 AFFECTED

The Imperial Japanese Army and Navy authorities in a joint proclamation issued today, announced the restriction of residences and places of business of stateless refugees in Shanghai to a designated area comprising sections of the Wayside and Yangtzepoo districts as from May 18. By stateless refugees are meant those European refugees who have arrived in Shanghai since 1937.

The designated area is bordered on the west by the line connecting Chaoufoong, Muirhead and Dent Roads; on the east by Yangtzepoo Creek; on the south by the line connecting East Seward, Muirhead and Wayside Roads, and on the north by the boundary of the International Settlement.

The statement of The Imperial Japanese Army and Navy authorities issued yesterday in connection with the proclamation follows:

"The Proclamation issued today by the Commanders-in-Chief of the Imperial Japanese Army and Navy in the Shanghai area hereafter restricts the residence and business of the local stateless refugees within a limited area.

"This measure is motivated by military necessity, and is, therefore, not an arbitrary action intended to oppress their legitimate occupation. It is even contemplated to safeguard so far as possible their place of residence as well as their livelihood in the designated area. Therefore, the stateless refugees to whom this Proclamation applies must, as a

PROCLAMATION

Concerning Restriction Of Residence and Business of Stateless Refugees

(I) Due to military necessity places of residence and business of the stateless refugees in the Shanghai area shall hereafter be restricted to the undermentioned area in the International Settlement.

East of the line connecting Chaoufoong Road, Muirhead Road and Dent Road;

West of Yangtzepoo Creek;

North of the line connecting East Seward Road, Muirhead Road and Wayside Road; and

South of the boundary of the International Settlement.

(II) The stateless refugees at present residing and/or carrying on business in the districts other than the above area shall remove their places of residence and/or business into the area designated above by May 18, 1943.

Permission must be obtained from the Japanese authorities for the transfer, sale, purchase or lease of the rooms, houses, shops or any other establishments, which are situated outside the designated area and now being occupied or used by the stateless refugees.

(III) Persons other than the stateless refugees shall not remove into the area mentioned in Article I without permission of the Japanese authorities.

(IV) Persons who will have violated this Proclamation or obstructed its enforcement shall be liable to severe punishment.

Commander-in-Chief of the
Imperial Japanese Army in the Shanghai Area.

Commander-in-Chief of the
Imperial Japanese Navy in the Shanghai Area.

February 18, 1943.

Japanese Urged To Help In Changing Residences With Stateless Refugees

The local Japanese community is requested to understand fully the significance of the proclamation issued today by the Commanders-in-Chief of the Imperial Japanese Army

The pronouncement was signed by General Yasugi Okamura. Peering closer, Lily read his title under her breath – *Commander-in-Chief of the Imperial Japanese Army*. But the message made no sense to her. Who were "stateless refugees?" Why were they being ordered to move to Hongkew, that horrible place she had visited with Pop? And what did any of this have to do with her or her parents? All she knew was that Pop was upset, and Mom looked just as distraught as she read the headlines and then looked up at her husband.

Lily and all of the Jewish refugees in Shanghai wondered where they would be able to go to find a safe place to live. This cartoon appeared in the *Shanghai Evening Post*.

"It doesn't say the word *Jews* anywhere here," Mom said, pointing at the newspaper.

Pop shook his head. "There's no question who this proclamation is intended for, Erna. We are the *stateless refugees*. All Jewish families arriving in Shanghai after 1937 are being ordered to move to Hongkew."

"It's just like when Hitler came to power," Mom whispered.

(left) In 1943, the newspapers reported that Jewish refugees were ordered to move into the Hongkew ghetto.

"We were fools to think that we were safe here," Pop replied. "Jews are not safe anywhere in the world."

Just then her parents looked around, realizing that Lily and Susie were at the table, listening and watching their exchange, their eyes widening with every word that was spoken.

"Go home, Susie," Pop said. "Go to your family. I'm sure your parents will want to talk to you about this."

Silently, Susie stood from the table. She gave Lily a quick hug

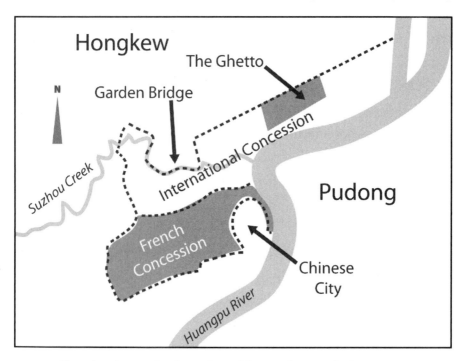

Shanghai during the Second World War: the French Concession
was separated from Hongkew by the Garden Bridge.

before bolting out the door. Lily had not moved. Her cardboard theater was still in her hands, and she dropped it now on the table and leaned toward her parents, confused and questioning. "I don't understand…" she began.

Pop grasped Lily's hands and brought his face close to hers. "We're moving, Lily," he said hoarsely. "Not so far this time, my darling. But we'll have to pack our things and clear out of this apartment."

Mom choked back some tears and covered her mouth with her hand. Lily still didn't understand what all of this meant. "Why do we have to move, Pop? We haven't done anything." In the back of her mind was the cloudy memory of a similar conversation that she had once had in Vienna with her mother.

"Remember we've talked about how Germany and Japan are friends?" Pop replied, choosing his words carefully. "These orders for the Jews to move probably come from Germany – from Hitler."

Lily shook her head. "But why is the Japanese army following Hitler's orders? We're not in Germany."

Pop sat back in his chair and glanced at his wife. "Japan is just playing it safe, not wanting to do anything to upset the Nazis in Europe. But don't worry," he added quickly, seeing the look of despair on Lily's face. "We're all going there together – Stella, Walter, Nini, Poldi, and Willi. What do I always tell you?"

"As long as the family is together, everything will be okay," Lily replied, repeating Pop's mantra but finding little comfort in the words.

Chapter 8

Lily could not fall asleep that night as her mind raced with thoughts of the recent turn of events. It still made no sense to her that Jewish families were being ordered to leave their homes and move to another part of Shanghai. Why was being Jewish such a problem? Even though her family was not all that observant, Lily loved being Jewish. She looked forward to the festivals that her family celebrated. She even enjoyed going to the synagogue with her parents and listening to the prayers that the rabbi recited. Why was this religion that she loved causing her so much trouble? That she would never understand.

And then there was Hongkew – that awful, dirty place she had visited with her father. All she could think about were the two little children she had met there and how hungry they were. Hongkew was a wasteland, a part of Shanghai that looked as if it had been thrown away or forgotten. Lily couldn't imagine how anyone survived in that place.

She pulled her blankets up closer to her chin and stared into the darkness, trying to think clearly. *Maybe this move won't be so bad,* she said to herself. *After all, we have already moved before. It might take time to adjust, but we can do it.* Coming here to Shanghai had worked out pretty well, so far. Their apartment was much tinier than their home had been in Vienna, but that didn't bother Lily much. She had her family here and her best friend.

So why did she have this uneasy creeping fear that would not go away? Why was her stomach all knotted up? And why was her body shaking even now as she lay in bed longing for sleep to take her away from all these thoughts and worries? Maybe it was something else, something her parents were not telling her. The words they had spoken sounded reassuring – *we'll be safe; our family will be together* – but their faces told another story.

As Lily waited, longing for sleep to claim her, she heard her parents whispering, as they often did from their bed across the room. Usually their muted conversation helped lull Lily to sleep. But when she heard her name in the darkness, she froze, every muscle in her body alert as she strained to hear what it was that Mom and Pop were saying.

"I couldn't tell Lily everything I heard," Pop began. "I didn't want to frighten her any more than necessary." He paused here, his breath shallow as he struggled to find the words to continue. "The newspaper article said that a Nazi colonel has come here from Germany. Joseph Meisinger is his name. They call him the 'Butcher of Warsaw.' I can only imagine how he got such a name. The rumors are that he's here now to deal with the Jews who managed to slip out of the Nazis' grasp in Europe. He's calling us 'the ones that got away.' There's talk that Meisinger's behind the order to move us into this ghetto."

It was the first time that her father had used that word – *ghetto* – to describe Hongkew. The box under Mom's bed was full of letters that described the horrible places their relatives had been sent to in Europe. Is that what was going to happen to Lily and her parents? Were the Jews of Shanghai going to be imprisoned? Was Hongkew about to become *their* ghetto?

"It may start like this, but what will come next?" Mom was whispering now. "We've heard of the concentration camps back home. Jews are disappearing into places where they are never heard from again. Is that going to be our fate too, after having come so far from Vienna?"

The memory of an old conversation rose in Lily's mind. What was the word that Mom had used when she spoke of family members being sent away? *Relocated.* That was it! Now her mind raced with a new fear. It was hard enough to imagine a ghetto – a place where you couldn't come and go as you liked and where conditions were horrible. But from the little that Lily knew about concentration camps, those places were gruesome. Uncle Willi was the one who had told

Lily that European Jews were being tortured and even killed in these places. Had her relatives been *relocated* to places like that? And is that what was going to happen to her and her parents? Lily began to shake again, a slow tremor that moved through her, from her arms down to her legs and into her feet.

"I think it might be best if Lily didn't come with us," Pop finally said.

What was that? Lily must have misunderstood these new whispers that came from her parents' side of the room. Where else was she going to go, if not with her parents? Lily strained to hear what her father was saying.

"Mother Lawler has offered to take Lily into the Missionary Home and raise her there. I think this might be a better alternative to having her come with us. We don't know what's going to happen in Hongkew. At least we know she'll be safe with the missionaries."

Lily had had enough. She sprang from her bed and in two steps was by her parents' side, trembling with new horror as she confronted them. "What are you saying, Pop? How can you think of leaving me behind?"

Neither parent moved or said a word.

"Mom, say something! I won't go anywhere without you. You can't leave me here."

Still her parents said nothing.

"If you really love me, you won't leave me here!" Lily hurled these charges at her parents. "Don't you care what happens to me? Don't you care if I'm all alone?" On and on she ranted and yelled, accusing her parents of abandoning her, being selfish, thinking only of themselves. The tears were streaming down Lily's cheeks now as she clutched her arms around her small body and stood shivering and helpless by her parents' bed.

Finally, Pop rose and encircled her in his arms. "Shhh, there, there," he whispered. "Calm down, my darling child. Stop shaking."

Lily would not be quieted. "I won't go to the Missionary Home. I won't go anywhere without you. You can't send me away, Pop," she continued. "You said that the family would stay together."

Lily was terrified at the thought of going to Hongkew – this ghetto – or perhaps worse. But as scary as Hongkew was to her, it was even more terrifying to imagine being left behind. That was simply unthinkable.

"We're just trying to do what is best for you, Lily." Mom joined them on the floor. The three of them stood in a huddled embrace in the cold and darkness of the small apartment.

"Then keep me with you," pleaded Lily. "That's what's best. I don't care what happens in Hongkew. I'll do anything to stay with you. Don't send me away."

There was a long pause. Lily didn't know what she would do if she couldn't convince her parents to take her with them into the ghetto. She would never stay with Mother Lawler; that was clear. As kind as the missionaries were, they were not her family. She would run away from the Missionary Home. She would disobey all the rules. She would refuse to eat. She would find a way back to her parents, no matter what.

Though it was dark, Lily could sense her Mom and Pop staring at one another above her head, agonizing over this unbearable choice. All the while, Lily clutched her parents, praying that they would reverse their decision and keep her with them. Finally, her father took one more breath, and she closed her eyes.

"All right, Lily," Pop said, struggling to speak. "You'll stay with us – with Mom and with me and the rest of the family. We'll go to live in Hongkew, together."

Lily was not quite convinced. "Promise me, Pop. Say it," she commanded.

Her parents bent in the darkness so that their faces were close to hers. Lily could make out the worry lines streaked across Pop's forehead, and the tears that streamed down Mom's face, and she held her breath once more. And then, in unison they replied, "We promise."

Chapter 9

March, 1943

Lily had barely adjusted to the announcement that her family would be moving to Hongkew when, a few weeks later, Willi burst into their apartment early in the morning. With hardly so much as a nod to Lily, he began pacing the small room.

"The Nazis have arrived. There was a parade yesterday on the Bund. Dozens, maybe hundreds of soldiers marched down the street – like they owned it! Swinging their rifles, stomping their boots on the ground, showing off their uniforms!" Willi was talking so fast that Lily had trouble catching every word. But the ones she heard were terrifying.

"Nazis! In Shanghai!" Mom's hand flew up to her throat as she sank onto a chair.

"It's Meisinger," said Pop. "The one I told you was here. After Hitler, he's one of the top commanders. He must be behind this demonstration."

"This was just one unit. Who knows how many more are coming?" Willi was still pacing, head down, hands clenched at his side.

"Fritz, what's happening?" Mom barely squeaked the words out.

"Did you see them, Willi? Did you actually *see* the Nazis? What did they look like?"

At the sound of Lily's voice, Willi came to an abrupt stop. He looked up, startled, as if he had forgotten Lily was there. Then he glanced at her parents before replying. "I wasn't at the parade," he said, carefully. "Nini and Poldi told me about it."

"But what are they doing here?" Lily suddenly felt cold. Her teeth were chattering and her hands felt numb. The upcoming move into Hongkew was all Lily had thought about in the preceding weeks. That was scary enough. But this talk of Nazis in Shanghai was more than she could imagine. And Willi didn't look like he was teasing her with scary stories. From the look on his face, Lily knew that this time, what he said was real.

"It's just rumors, right now," said Willi, more slowly this time. "Some people say that the Nazis are plotting to take over Shanghai."

"It's not enough to move us into a ghetto. Now, Hitler is coming after us," Mom said.

"No one really knows why the Nazis have come, Lily." This time, it was Pop who was speaking. "Just like Willi says – all rumors."

"But could they do it, Pop? Could they take over Shanghai?"

At this, Willi jumped in again. "Here's the thing," he said. "The Japanese aren't letting these Nazis get away with this. Poldi told me that when the Nazi troops were on the Bund, a group of Japanese soldiers actually surrounded them and marched them away. The Japanese aren't giving up Shanghai so quickly – not even to Hitler."

Pop moved toward Lily and touched her face. His hand was warm against her icy cheek. "You see, my darling? Shanghai is still safe. We're all still safe."

"I need to get to work," said Willi, moving toward the door. "I'll bring more news later, if I can."

With that, he headed out. Lily followed soon after. She needed to talk to Susie. But she didn't have a chance for a real conversation with her friend until a few more days had passed. That afternoon, the two girls sat on the stoop in front of Susie's apartment building. It was nearing the end of March and the sharp sting of winter was beginning to subside. Warmer winds had picked up, as if they were trying to push the colder air away as quickly as possible. Lily's winter jacket had been exchanged for a lighter one that she had buttoned halfway up.

Susie already knew about the Nazi parade on the Bund. "I don't think moving into Hongkew is worrying my parents as much as all the talk about Hitler's soldiers being here," she said.

Lily nodded. Willi had returned to their apartment several more times with news about the possibility of a Nazi takeover in Shanghai.

"Willi said that they're talking about loading Jewish refugees onto freighters and setting us out to drift on the Yangtze River – just letting us starve out there." She shuddered.

"I know," replied Susie. "My father heard that the Nazis promised the Japanese army that they could take all of our possessions if they got rid of us."

What possessions? Mom's sewing machine? Most of the valuable things that Lily's family owned had been left behind in Vienna. The same was true for most Jewish families. This sounded ridiculous. Lily didn't know what to believe anymore. "My Pop says that the Japanese army will never go along with Hitler. Both of them want to be the strongest. But how long can the Japanese keep pushing back and saying no?"

"Maybe moving us into Hongkew will be enough. At least for now…" The rest of Susie's thought was left unspoken. Her voice trailed off and the two girls sat quietly.

Lily was the first one to break the silence. "When I ask my parents about how true all this stuff is, they say nothing's going to happen. But they're just saying that so I won't be scared."

"All the grown-ups say one thing when they think kids aren't listening, and then say another thing as soon as we ask them a question."

"Susie, what do you think about moving into the ghetto? Are you scared?" On every lamppost up and down the street, there were signs declaring that the "stateless refugees" of Shanghai were being ordered into Hongkew. No matter where Lily looked there was a reminder of the upcoming move – as if they needed one! It was all anyone talked about these days.

"A little," replied Susie.

"Me too!" Lily had told Susie everything about her visit into Hongkew with her father. "When I told you how awful that place was, I never thought we'd actually have to live there."

"I didn't either."

How was it possible that Shanghai, the city that had once saved Lily's family, was beginning to feel like enemy territory? Lily didn't want to think about ghettos or the possibility of Nazi soldiers coming after them. She didn't want to think about being set adrift and starving in the middle of nowhere. She didn't want to think about any of this.

"Do you suppose we'll live close to each other in Hongkew?" Susie's question broke through Lily's silence.

Lily smiled faintly. "We'd better!"

Susie returned the smile. "Maybe my parents can talk to yours and see if it's possible."

"Sure," Lily replied half-heartedly. As much as she longed to be close to her best friend in Hongkew, she knew that this would be the last thing on Pop's mind, as he tried to find a place for the family to live.

Chapter 10

Pop began to search for an apartment in Hongkew the very next day while Lily and her mother stayed home to pack up their belongings. Even though the Jews of Shanghai had been allowed three months within which they had to move, Pop thought it best that they find a place as soon as possible.

"Think about it," he said. "Thousands of people are going to be looking for a place to live. Hongkew is already packed with Chinese citizens. The sooner we find an apartment, the better."

Every day for weeks, he left home even earlier than usual to go and search for a place. And every day he returned, shoulders drooped and shaking his head. It seemed that many other Jewish families had also started their search for a new apartment in Hongkew. "It's harder than I thought it would be," he said. "You can't believe how terrible some of the places are. And tiny! Some are not big enough for Lily's dolls, never mind a family of three. Right now, it seems impossible." His voice trailed off into silence.

Lily had already seen how dark and tiny a room could be in Hongkew. Was that the kind of apartment that was in store for them?

"A toilet," Mom pleaded. "I'm not asking for much, and we don't need a lot of space. But please try to find a place that has a proper toilet."

Lily knew that the alternative to the proper toilet Mom wanted was a bucket toilet that most Chinese and many Jewish families had. Every morning, coolies would enter homes and carry these communal buckets to the side of the road, full and slopping over the sides. They would empty them into large wagons that they pulled down the street. The wagons were called honey carts, which always made Lily laugh. "It's such a pretty name for such a disgusting thing," she would say. Brown liquid oozed out of these carts and the stench that followed them could choke the strongest person. Lily didn't want to complain or ask for things from her parents, who already looked so worried, but like her mother, she too hoped for a decent toilet.

Lily's aunts and uncles were also looking for places to live in Hongkew. And like Lily and her parents, they were having a difficult time. They shared their stories many evenings when they would gather around the table in Lily's apartment.

"They're asking a fortune for a rat-infested hole in the wall. It's criminal," Aunt Nini wailed one evening, echoing the sentiments of everyone in the room. "We looked at a house where the plaster is crumbling and the roof has so many holes in it, there may as well not be one! What's more, there are already twenty families living there, in a space that's meant for only two or three!" Poldi sat quietly at the table. These days he just looked troubled by everything that was happening. Not only would Aunt Nini and Uncle Poldi be forced out of their home, they were also being ordered to give up their business.

Like all Jewish businesses in the French Concession, their club would soon be under Japanese management.

"I'll look for work in Hongkew once we've found a place to live," Pop said.

Mom hoped that she would be able to continue working at the convent. "I don't know what restrictions we'll have to live under," she said, "but perhaps, if I show the authorities that I have a good and steady job here, they'll let me go out of the ghetto every day."

Aunt Stella and Uncle Walter owned a coffee shop in Frenchtown called Café de Paris. In the evenings it featured live entertainment.

Like Nini and Poldi, Lily's Aunt Stella and Uncle Walter were also being forced to close their coffee shop. They were searching for an apartment in Hongkew that would also house Willi. Willi looked worried about the turn of events. His usual teasing and joking with Lily had stopped. She wondered what was worse; having Willi bombard her with his scary stories, or watching him withdraw into silence.

These evening gatherings continued for several more weeks until Pop walked into the apartment one night with the news that he had found a place. "I think we're luckier than most," he said as he sat facing his wife and daughter at the table. Lily was now being fully included in their conversations. The whispered discussions late into the night had stopped. She was ten and no longer the little child she had been when the family had first arrived in Shanghai. She was growing up fast, perhaps faster than any young person should have to. Her parents had finally decided that she could be part of their debates and their decisions. She sat up in her chair and leaned forward, waiting to hear the news of where they would be living.

"There's an old Chinese middle school in Hongkew that's now being run by a group trying to help Jewish families find housing in the ghetto." Pop spelled out the initials of the organization – S.A.C.R.A. "It stands for Shanghai Ashkenazi Collaboration Relief Association," he said. "The school hasn't been used for some time, so the classrooms have been turned into apartments. Every single inch of space is needed now that so many Jews are going to be crowding into that part of the city."

"How big?" whispered Mom.

"Tiny!" Pop shrugged his shoulders. "It's still just one room and smaller than this one." He gestured around their apartment. "But we'll have it all to ourselves. That's a good thing."

Lily couldn't imagine living with her parents in a room that was even smaller than this cramped space. But she did not speak out. After convincing her parents to take her with them into the ghetto, she had vowed not to complain about anything.

"It's selling for a fortune," Pop continued.

"All our savings?" Mom whispered these words and Pop nodded.

"It will cost pretty much everything we have to purchase the flat. But at least we have a place."

"And…?" Mom leaned forward, her eyes pleading for an answer to the one question she still had.

Pop finally allowed a small smile to cross his face. He placed his hand reassuringly on top of hers. "A real flush toilet, Erna," he said. "We were able to get some special consideration because we have a child. These apartments are reserved for families." Mom clapped her hands together and sprang from the table to give her husband a quick hug.

Lily finally spoke up. "You see?" she said. "I knew there was another reason for you to take me with you into Hongkew. You can thank *me* for the toilet!"

The three of them finally dissolved into some welcome laughter.

Her family had no idea what they were going to be facing in Hongkew, and yet the news of a flush toilet had given them some sense of pleasure. *It's amazing how something so small can be so important,* thought Lily.

"And there's more, Lily," Pop said, facing his daughter. "You'll go to school in the ghetto, but this time, it's going to be a Jewish school. It's not far from our new apartment."

"Will Susie be there?" The thought of a Jewish school was something new and interesting.

Pop nodded. "Yes, and hopefully you'll also make new friends."

Lily sat back in her chair and looked around the room. Several suitcases sat in a corner, already packed and ready for the move. Her books were in a separate pile; she would take those with her, as well. But aside from their clothing and some other personal items, they had very little here that would be going with them into their new apartment. Some of their things would have to be sold off or simply left behind. With a smaller space, there would be no room for the wardrobe that sat in one corner, or some of Mom's dishes and pots. Even Lily's bed would remain behind, replaced with a small, roll-away cot. The treadle sewing machine would come with them, of course. Mom was not going to leave that – especially after the journey it had already made from Vienna. But none of those things mattered to Lily. What mattered was that she was going to stay with her parents and her aunts and uncles.

Chapter 11

The move was scheduled for two days later. Willi was there to help Pop load their belongings onto a rickshaw that her parents had hired. The rickshaw driver smiled a toothless grin as he carried their suitcases out the door, grunting and bending under the load. He was so thin and wiry; he looked as if he might snap in two from the weight of their luggage. Pop and Willi piled their meager furnishings, boxes, linens, and dishes onto the rickshaw, tying everything securely with heavy rope. The sewing machine was the last to go, claiming a special place at the top of the load. Willi and Pop were going to walk behind this cart while Lily and her mother rode on another rickshaw. They'd meet up at their new apartment where they would unload their belongings.

"Good-bye, Mrs. Kinecky," Lily called to her upstairs neighbor.

"We're moving in a few days too, Lily," Mrs. Kinecky replied from the top of the stairs. "But only one of the dogs is coming with us. No space. We've had to find homes for the other three. I hope they'll be okay. I hope we'll all be okay," she added.

Lily nodded and waved. She would miss the Kineckys, even if their dogs had kept her up many nights. Lily glanced across the hall where her Chinese neighbors had lived. They'd disappeared weeks earlier, and Lily had no idea where they were. Finally, she looked around the nearly empty room that had been home for the past four years. She walked over to the spot in the middle of the room where the table and chairs had stood, and glanced at the balcony where she'd dyed her hair, recalling once more how Oma had fallen chasing her. She didn't realize that her father had followed her into the flat.

"It's just four walls until you put your things in it and make it a home," said Pop. "We'll make a new home in Hongkew, Lily." Lily nodded, not trusting herself to speak. And with that, she followed her father out the door and climbed into the rickshaw.

Normally, a rickshaw ride would have been a treat for Lily. It was always fun to sit on the soft cushions of the carriage, bouncing this way and that, as the driver pulled you along the road. The excitement had always been in the close calls and near misses as the carriage swerved around the people, cars, and bicycles that filled the streets of Shanghai. Sometimes, you could reach out and almost touch the vehicle that pulled up next to you. But today, there was little joy as Lily moved along the Bund, away from the French Concession.

Today, it appeared as if all the traffic was heading one way, and that was toward Hongkew.

The Garden Bridge, which crossed over Suzhou Creek, was jammed with traffic. Lily's rickshaw moved at a snail's pace, crawling toward their new home. It was accompanied by a procession of rickshaws, wagons, cars, trucks, and people. It reminded Lily of the Passover story of Moses and the Jewish people who had escaped from the evil pharaoh. They had left Egypt in long caravans as they moved out into the desert. Those Jews eventually ended up in the Promised Land. Lily was afraid that Hongkew was not going to be a happy destination.

The area designated for the Jews of Shanghai was approximately one square mile. One hundred thousand Chinese citizens were already crammed into Hongkew along with more than five thousand Jewish refugees who had settled there from the very beginning. And they were about to be joined by an additional fifteen thousand Jews!

Lily's rickshaw wound its way toward the ghetto. Having seen Hongkew with her father months earlier, she thought she knew what to expect. But things had changed dramatically since then. A checkpoint, manned by Japanese soldiers with long rifles pointed at the Jewish refugees, now stood in the center of the Garden Bridge. They were just like the soldiers Lily had seen in that parade on the Bund, the day after the bombing of Pearl Harbor. There didn't appear to be any Nazi soldiers in sight. That was a relief. But these Japanese soldiers were threatening enough as they shouted orders for the Jews to pick up their pace.

Once across the bridge, Lily could see that the streets were now barricaded with barbed wire fences. She shuddered as her rickshaw passed the sharp wire barriers, knowing that these blockades had only one purpose, and that was to keep the Jewish refugees imprisoned inside. As the rickshaw made its way up the road, Lily gazed at her surroundings with new curiosity. It had been one thing to visit the ghetto for a morning with her Pop. It was quite another to realize that this dark and dirty place was her new home.

Buildings leaned dangerously on the ones next to them and looked as if they might fall down with the slightest gust of wind. Everywhere she looked, Lily saw smashed-out windows. Broken glass lay in piles, along with rotting wood and tiles. The smells were even worse than Lily remembered. Gutters overflowed with human waste and garbage. Lily reached up to plug her nose, but it was impossible to filter out the disgusting smells. Mom coughed next to her and gasped for air. Her face was pale and Lily quickly turned away. She was trying to stay brave and strong, and it didn't help to see Mom looking so distressed.

The last time Lily had been here, she was the one who had stared at the citizens of Hongkew as they walked on the streets and lay inside dark passageways. Today, it felt as if all the Chinese men, women, and children were gawking at her and the other Jews who were invading their neighborhood. They looked puzzled, as if they couldn't understand who these new arrivals were and how they were all going to cram into this tiny area. Lily crouched lower in the rickshaw, but it was impossible to hide from the open stares.

With each passing minute, the roads became more rutted under the wheels of the rickshaw making the passage even slower. Their coolie grunted under the load and bent lower as he pulled Lily and Mom closer to their final destination. After more twists and curves, the rickshaw made one final turn onto East Yuhang Road and came to a stop in front of number 826. They had arrived at their new home. The two-story former school looked decent enough from the outside – better than most of the buildings on the rundown street. That was a relief! With a deep breath, Lily jumped from the rickshaw, turned to help her mother down, and began to help with the bags and boxes that arrived just after them on the second cart. Their apartment was on the second floor of the building, next to a wide stairwell. It did not take long to unload their furnishings into the tiny one-room apartment. Willi took off as soon as the luggage was in place. He was helping Stella and Walter move into the house on the other side of Hongkew where the three of them would be living. Nini and Poldi's place was nearby. The family was going to be together in the ghetto, just as Pop had promised. And miraculously, Susie's apartment was also going to be close. This was all comforting to Lily as she helped carry their belongings into their new flat.

Nearly fifteen thousand Jewish refugees were forced into the Hongkew ghetto, crossing over the Garden Bridge and leaving their homes in Frenchtown far behind.

Lily was finally able to take a good look around. The room had one small window on the wall opposite the door. *No more balcony*, she thought. There was a space in the corner for Mom and Pop's bed and a spot across from them for Lily's cot. A small electric burner sat close to the window. The table and chairs were placed in the center of the room, leaving just enough space to walk around without banging into the walls. Clothing, pots, pans, and other smaller items were piled on a shelf to one side. And that was it!

"You see," Pop said as he placed Mom's sewing machine up against the wall under the window. "Everything will be fine here. It's a bit small, but cozy, don't you think?"

Next door, they could hear the voices of adults rising and falling mixed with the sound of someone, a woman, crying. The walls were so thin here; there was even less privacy than in their previous flat. Mom said nothing, though her eyes looked gloomier than ever. She ran her finger down one wall and brought it away caked with grit and grease. Then she set her mouth in a tight line.

A soft knock at the door startled Lily. When Mom opened it, an elderly Chinese woman stood there with her head slightly bowed. Lily had never seen so many wrinkles on the face of one person. She watched as Mom pointed to the walls of the apartment and exchanged a few words of broken Chinese with the stranger. Finally, the old woman nodded and grinned, her wrinkles folding back on her face like a paper fan.

Mom pulled the woman into the apartment. "We need to clean this place up," she said. "I don't care how small it is, I am not sleeping in a room that is so filthy. Fritz, you go start to look for work. Lily, go off and play." Mom nodded toward the Chinese woman. "This *amah* is going to get this place ready for us to live in it."

Back in Frenchtown, the amahs had always been there to help clean their apartment. But Lily didn't know how this wrinkled old woman was going to scrub away the layers of muck that had built up on these walls over what looked like years of neglect. For now, she was happy to be let out of the task of cleaning. She kissed her parents and ran out the door. It was time to explore this place more closely.

Down the hall was a series of apartment doors. There was also one other door leading to the all-important flush toilets. Her family would share these toilets with the floor of apartments. But that didn't matter. At least there would be no buckets to remove every day. Lily wandered down the stairs onto the first floor. It looked just like the one upstairs – a series of apartments leading off of the long hallway. She walked out the door of the building and turned left. Next to the apartment building was a smaller wooden structure that housed the kitchen. There was a gas stove inside that would also be shared with all the families. *If the little burner in our apartment doesn't work, at least we'll be able to cook in here,* thought Lily. A smaller room in the back had a shower. Pop had told her that men and women were assigned to use the shower room at different times of the day. Lily was wondering who her neighbors were going to be when someone tapped her on the shoulder. She whirled around. A young boy was standing in front of her.

"Hi. My name is Harry. I saw you move into the SACRA this morning. I live upstairs too, right next to you."

Harry looked about eleven or twelve, a year or two older than Lily. He had brown, tousled hair, and he kicked at some stones on the path as he waited for her to reply. It was funny that he referred to the apartment as the SACRA, Lily thought. Those were the initials of the organization that Pop had said managed the former school building and that was trying to help Jews in the new ghetto. SACRA – it was as good a name as any for her new home – and made it sound nicer than it really was.

"My name's Lily," she finally replied. "Have you lived here a long time?"

Harry shook his head. "Only about a month. We moved in right after the notice came out about the designated area. Most of the people in the building are new as well. I can show you around, if you want."

Lily was pleased. It was good to talk to someone close to her own age who already knew his way around the building and its surroundings. Harry pointed out the yard in the back with a huge haystack in the middle for climbing.

"It's fun," he said, "as long as you don't mind the bugs that crawl in and out of the hay. You get used to being bitten." Lily shuddered. Bugs were not her favorite.

"What's that over there?" She pointed at a long, concrete building behind the kitchen and off to one side.

"It was a bomb shelter, I think," Harry replied. "I don't know what it's used for these days."

The only knowledge of bombs that Lily had was the destruction of Pearl Harbor. Her mind returned to Harry and the tour. "What about back there?" This time, she pointed to a wall that ran the length of the back of the building and enclosed the yard on one side.

"There's a Japanese army unit stationed on the other side of the wall. You can see the soldiers from the top of the haystack, along with a radio tower off to one side. I guess they're there to keep an eye on us – make sure we don't leave Hongkew." Harry formed his hands into an imaginary pair of binoculars, pointed them right at Lily, and laughed. "I don't know where they think we're going to go."

Lily shuddered again as she glanced at the wall. It was disturbing to think that there really were soldiers positioned on the other side to watch the movements of the Jewish refugees. It made her feel even more like a prisoner.

By the time Lily had finished her tour of the building with Harry, it was starting to get dark. She said good-bye to her new friend and ran back up the stairs to her apartment. The *amah* was just finishing the last of the cleaning. She looked up at Lily and smiled her wrinkled smile once more before accepting a few cents from Mom and turning to leave. Lily had to admit that the small room looked much better than when they had moved in a few hours ago.

"As soon as I have a bit of time, I'm going to get some curtains for that window," Mom said. "You see, Lily? It's going to feel like a home very soon."

Lily hoped that was true.

Paper money was used in Shanghai, even for amounts as small as twenty cents.

Chapter 12

That night, Lily slept better and deeper than she could have ever imagined, and she woke up refreshed the next morning, ready for school. Mom and Pop, on the other hand, looked exhausted. There were deep shadows under Pop's eyes, and Mom's skin was pale and a bit yellow. But if they'd had a whispered conversation late into the night, Lily had not heard a word.

She pulled the blankets up over her bed, gulped a quick breakfast of cold rice in milk, and flew out the door ahead of her mother. Mom would accompany Lily to school this first morning so she could introduce her to the teachers and get her settled in her new class. Lily's emotions rode up and down like the merry-go-round she had ridden on as a child, back in Vienna. She hadn't thought about the Prater Amusement Park in years. On the one hand, she was excited to be going to a school for Jewish students. There would be no missionaries here who would try to convert her. It would be fun to meet new children; Lily was looking forward to that. But would she fit in? Would she make new friends? Would she do well in this new school? She hoped no one would try to call her Lillian. She hated her full name. She was Lily. That's what she would insist on being called. Still, all these unknowns had her stomach tightening and letting go just like it did on the wooden horses that circled the statue of the giant Chinese man in the center of that ride back in Austria.

"First days are always difficult," Pop had said earlier that morning, as if reading her mind. Pop had been on his way out the door to look for work. He kissed her lightly on the forehead and squeezed her arm reassuringly. "Learn something new today, Lily," he had said. "And then you can tell me about it when I get home."

The Shanghai Jewish Youth Association School – at 627 East Yuhang Road – was only a couple of blocks down the street from where Lily lived. On the way, Mom talked to her about her new school and the wealthy Jewish family who had built it. They had come from India more than a hundred years earlier. "Horace Kadoorie built this place here in Hongkew," Mom said as they reached the door of the school. "Everyone just calls it the Kadoorie School."

Lily entered through the double doors at the front of the building. Inside, it was cool and dimly lit. Their feet clattered on the wooden floor as she and her mother walked past several open classrooms before entering the office of the headmistress.

Miss Lucie Hartwich rose from her desk chair to greet Lily. "We're happy to have you here," she said, extending her hand. "Many of the students are new to our Kadoorie School, just like you, Lily. So you have nothing to worry about."

Lily returned the handshake, solemnly. Miss Hartwich sounded welcoming enough, but she had a stern face that did nothing to reassure her new student. At least the headmistress had called her Lily. That was a good beginning. With one last good-bye to Mom, Lily followed the headmistress down the hall to her classroom.

The lesson was already underway. Several girls and boys were gathered around a large map of the world at the front of the room. The teacher, Mr. Tobias, stopped the lesson when he saw Miss Hartwich at the door.

"Attention, class. I think we have a new student joining us today."

Lily stepped forward, nudged by the headmistress. "I'm Lily Toufar." She stuttered her name out loud and was instantly surrounded by a group of students.

"I'm Hazel. Where are you living?"

"I'm Rhea. Do you have any brothers or sisters?"

"My name is Mabel. I think you're the shortest one in the class."

"I'm Daisy. Don't mind Mabel. She isn't being mean. You can sit in the empty spot next to me."

One after another, the girls in the class introduced themselves to Lily. The boys hung back, watching the others crowd around this new student. Lily could barely keep the names straight, or where they all lived, or who their parents and siblings were. But by the time the introductions were over, she felt more at ease.

The teacher brought the class to order and continued with the lesson. "We're talking about how we all came to Shanghai," Mr. Tobias said. "Lily, would you like to come up to the map and show us where you came from?"

Lily rose from her desk and made her way to the front of the classroom. She stared at the map on the wall, searching first for Austria. It was halfway around the world from Shanghai. "My family came from Vienna," Lily began, pointing to the spot on the map. "We left in 1938 and traveled first by train here, to Genoa, Italy. Then we got on a ship that sailed along the Mediterranean Sea, through the Suez Canal past Africa, and around the tip of India." As she talked, she continued to trace the journey her family had made, realizing it was the first time she had actually plotted the voyage on a map. It was remarkable to see how far they had come – more than eight thousand miles! "Then we sailed past Singapore and the Philippines to Shanghai. It took us about four weeks, and we've been here ever since."

Mr. Tobias nodded his approval. "You'll find that I and many of your classmates made a similar journey," he said as Lily sat down.

The morning passed quickly. Lily moved from class to class, meeting her new teachers and discovering what she would be studying:

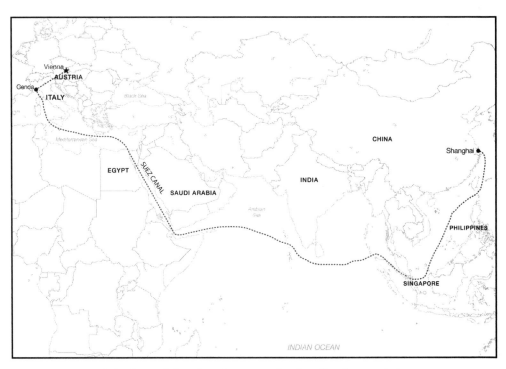

Lily showed the class the route that her family traveled.
First they went by train from Vienna to Genoa, and then by boat to
Shanghai, a journey that took more than a month.

geography with Mr. Tobias, along with geometry, science, literature, and Japanese. Miss Hartwich would teach French and music. All the subjects were familiar to Lily, except for Japanese, and that subject would be new for all the students because it was a recent requirement of the Japanese government. At recess, she and the other girls headed for the large grassy courtyard in the center of the u-shaped school building. They played hopscotch and skipped with a rope that was a collection of elastic bands knotted together. The girls taught Lily a Japanese skipping song that she quickly learned. "*Sa – ku – ra, sa – ku – ra.* Cherry blossoms, cherry blossoms, everywhere." She saw Susie in the distance and waved to her. They would catch up later. But for now, Lily wanted to be with her classmates and learn as much as she could about this new school. The girls were full of information they were only too happy to share.

"Watch out for Miss Hartwich," the girl named Rhea said. "She's tough and she'll give you the ruler across your knuckles if you're late or haven't got your work done."

Lily's instinct had been right about the headmistress. She would try to avoid her at all costs.

"Everyone likes the math teacher, Mr. Gassenheimer. And gym is pretty good," another child continued. She reminded Lily that her name was Mabel. "The gym teacher, Mr. Meyer, used to be a famous soccer player in Germany. But if you fall behind, he'll make you run ten more laps around this field."

Lily had never been very athletic, but now she knew she would have to try and keep up with the other students. By the time the day ended, Lily's head was buzzing. School had felt…*normal!* In fact, for most of the day, she had almost forgotten it was in the middle of a ghetto where she and thousands of Jewish families were imprisoned. If this was what Hongkew was going to be like, then Lily thought she could manage it. She headed out the door, her mind full of stories to tell Pop when he got home that night. The first person she bumped into was Harry, the boy from her new apartment building.

"How was your first day?" he asked.

"Pretty good, I think. It's hard to keep everyone's name straight and figure out all the work. But I think it's going to be okay."

"You'll sort it out soon enough," said Harry. "And wait until you hear about all the sports teams and activities we have. You can join soccer or badminton or even Scouts."

Lily, in the front row, second from right, joined the Jewish Scouts of Shanghai.

Lily wrinkled her nose. She would probably not be joining any sports teams, though Scouts did sound interesting. Lily and Harry fell into an easy conversation as they walked down the street to the SACRA. Even though it was only a few blocks to their apartment, the road was overflowing with people, making the route challenging. Lily was pushed and jostled on all sides by people who seemed in a hurry to get somewhere. She was just about to say something to Harry about the crowds when a young Chinese man pushed his way between them, grabbed the school bag off Harry's shoulder, and took off down the street. It happened in the blink of an eye.

"Hey, come back here!" Harry shouted. He sprinted off in pursuit of the thief.

For a second, Lily stood open-mouthed, then she tore after Harry. But keeping up with her friend was not easy. If it had been difficult to walk through the surge of people on the streets of Hongkew, it was even tougher to run through it. Harry darted this way and that, staying on the heels of the man who had stolen his bag. And somehow, Lily managed to keep them in sight. The three of them ran through several dimly lit alleyways and onto narrow cobblestone lanes. The young thief clearly knew every square inch of Hongkew. It was only when they emerged onto a larger street that Harry was finally able to overtake the thief and wrestle the bag away from him. Lily caught up with them in time to hear Harry explode with anger.

"Get lost," he shouted. "And if I see you again, you won't get off so easy!" The young man ran off without a backward glance.

Lily stood next to Harry, doubled over and panting. "Shouldn't we call the police?" she asked when she finally caught her breath.

Harry looked amused. "Police? Who do you think cares about something like this? Or about us? It happens all the time. I was stupid not to hold onto my things."

Instinctively, Lily pulled her own schoolbag closer to her chest and looked around. She had no idea where they were. She looked pleadingly at Harry.

"Come on. I'll lead you back home to the SACRA," he said. "Some adventure for your first day, don't you think?"

Lily smiled. "I'll remember this if that gym teacher ever makes me do extra laps in the school yard."

Lily and Harry made their way back to their apartment building. It was strange that the incident with the thief had not scared Lily. She had learned something on day one in Hongkew. She would have to be on her guard here in the ghetto and be ready to fight to survive. Perhaps this was one story that she would not share with her father.

Chapter 13

It took some time before Pop finally found work in the ghetto. Early every morning, long before Lily had arisen for school, Pop was out on the streets, searching for a business opportunity, errands he could run, anything that would earn some money for his family. And every night, he returned empty-handed.

"There are thousands like me searching for work," he explained to Lily as he tucked her into bed.

"You'll find something, Pop," she replied. "I just know you will."

Pop smiled down at his daughter. "I won't give up," he said firmly. "I can't give up!"

And then, one evening, Pop walked into the apartment with great news. The house Walter and Stella had purchased at the far end of Hongkew came with a small storefront on the main floor. Pop had decided to take the space and open a shoe store. "Everyone needs shoes," he said. His face lit up with a broad smile. "The rent I pay will help Walter out. With so many Jewish families here in the ghetto, I'm sure the store will do well. I'm going to call it 'Schuhhaus Paris' – The Paris Shoe House."

Lily laughed along with her father. It was such an elegant-sounding name.

"The truth is, it's a tiny space and rather dirty right now. But I'll clean it up and hire a couple of workers. Willi can join me, so it will be a family business." It was a night for Lily and her parents to celebrate.

But while Pop was easily able to go to work every day at his shoe store inside the Hongkew borders, Mom was finding work a more challenging experience. Jews were not permitted to leave the designated area, but Mom was desperately trying to hold on to her job at the convent back in Frenchtown. In order for her to leave the ghetto and get to work, she had to apply for a weekly pass card with a stamp that would be shown to the armed Japanese police who patrolled the Garden Bridge, separating Hongkew from the free area of Shanghai. These police stood under large banners that read:

STATELESS REFUGEES ARE PROHIBITED TO PASS
HERE WITHOUT PERMISSION.[3]

The man who issued those pass cards giving permission to leave the ghetto was a Japanese general whose name was Kanoh Ghoya. In the beginning, it had been fairly easy for Mom to get her card stamped

Pop, left, hung this painted glass sign in the window of his Hongkew shoe store.

by General Ghoya. And though she traveled for hours to and from her job, she was happy to leave the ghetto and get to work. All that began to change after several months had passed.

One Monday morning, Lily accompanied her mother to get her pass card stamped. Lily had complained of a headache that morning and Mom agreed to let her stay home from school. But rather than have her stay in the dank apartment all day, Mom had insisted that Lily come with her. "The fresh air will be good for you," she said. "And perhaps we'll buy a little sweet bun on the way home."

That was what persuaded Lily to peel herself off her cot and join her mother on the walk to the Stateless Refugees Affairs Bureau on Muirhead Road. Even though it was early in the morning and the office would not open for hours, the line wound its way down the street and around the corner. General Ghoya had not yet arrived, but Lily heard people whispering and wondering whether or not they would come away with the precious stamps that day.

"The General is as crazy as a bedbug," one woman said to the man standing next to her.

"Yes, last week, he threatened to shove my friend out the window," the man replied.

"My friend was thrown in jail for a night, just because Ghoya thought his English wasn't good enough," the woman continued.

"We'll know what mood he's in as soon as he turns the corner," someone else chimed in.

Lily wasn't sure she wanted to be there for any of this. Her head was still pounding with a headache and not even the promise of a treat was appealing at this point. She stepped closer to her mother. Finally, she heard a loud murmur that rippled through the crowd. General Ghoya was walking down the street and approaching the long line. Lily moved behind her mother where she was slightly hidden but could still get a good look at this man whom everyone was calling

It was dangerous to cross the Garden Bridge where Japanese guards were always on patrol.

crazy. The first thing she noticed was his height. *He's as short as I am,* she thought, marveling at how someone so small could wield so much power. Ghoya was a pint-sized menace, a thin man with slicked back hair and a permanent sneer on his face. As he passed by the silent line of refugees, he turned and shouted, "I'm the King of the Jews!" With a satisfied smile, he moved up the stairs and into his office.

"If you ask me, he looks more like a monkey," one of the Jewish refugees behind Lily whispered. Others in line snickered and nodded.

The line to the General's office moved slowly. Lily watched those who came out of the building after having faced him. Some clutched their pass cards to their chests and raised their faces to the sky, giving silent thanks for having received a stamp. Others hung their heads and slowly walked away. Lily tugged on her mother's sleeve. "Mom, what if you don't get your card stamped?" she asked as the line inched forward.

"I'll get the stamp, Lily."

"But what if you can't go to work?"

An elderly man standing in the line in front of Lily turned around. "No work, no money, no food on the table." He leaned closer. "And then, they throw you out on the street."

Mom pulled Lily under her arm. "I'll get the stamp," she repeated.

Hours went by and finally, Lily and her mother were about to stand before General Ghoya. Lily watched one more refugee ahead of them approach his desk. Ghoya stared at the Jewish man in front of him.

"I work at the Washing Road hospital across the bridge," the man said. His voice was low and quivered slightly. "I'm an orderly there." He had removed his hat and held it limply at his side.

He waited with his head bowed. Ghoya eyed him up and down and then leaned forward in his chair. "Liar!" he shouted. "You're one of the spies!"

The man looked up, startled. "No, no, I'm not a spy," he protested, weakly. "I'm an honest man. I must get to work so that I can feed my family and pay my rent."

"Spy!" Ghoya shouted again. "I'll have you jailed."

The man looked as if he was going to pass out. "No, please…" He clutched his hands together, pleadingly.

Ghoya had no patience for this. He jumped up, reached across his desk, and slapped the man hard across his face. "No pass! No pass!" Ghoya shrieked. The man nearly fell to his knees. Lily gasped out loud.

"Sh!" Mom hissed. "Not a sound." She stepped in front of Lily who could not resist peering around her mother to see what was happening.

The man grabbed his hat, which had fallen to the ground, and fled. His face was ghostly white except for a red palm print that was boldly visible on one cheek. Meanwhile, General Ghoya had straightened his tie and resumed his seat behind his desk.

Mom was next. She moved up in front of Ghoya, and Lily crept along behind her. Mom had dressed up that day. In fact, most of the refugees were wearing their best clothes, trying to impress this powerful and evil little man. Lily was trembling from head to toe. Having witnessed the man ahead of them, she was terrified that the General would come after Mom. She held her breath.

"I work in the Sacred Heart Hospital Convent," Mom began as she laid her pass card on the desk. "I teach embroidery and sewing to the young girls."

Lily was amazed at how calm her mother sounded. Her voice was confident and controlled. Ghoya stared down at the pass card and then up at Mom. Then he caught sight of Lily and he curled his lips into a sinister grin. Instinctively, she moved back behind her mother. Her head, which had been aching all day, was throbbing. Finally, after what felt like the longest pause, Ghoya reached for his stamp and pounded it down hard onto Mom's pass card.

"Pass for you!" he shouted as he tossed the card back to Mom. She and Lily fled from his office. They were safe, and more importantly, Mom had her precious stamp. The people still in the line eyed Mom enviously as she held her pass card triumphantly in the air.

"That went well today," Mom said as they started to walk away from the office. She still looked calm enough, but Lily could detect a slight quiver in her voice. "I think we both deserve that treat," Mom added.

Lily didn't trust herself to speak. But now that she was back on the street she felt as if she could breathe again. She was overjoyed that her mother would be able to get to her job outside of Hongkew. But her happiness was short-lived. The headache that had plagued her all morning was still there, though perhaps not quite as severe. Still, it reminded her that in a week, Mom would be back here in this line-up asking for another stamp. No one knew how long this would go on – or if things would get worse.

To work outside the ghetto, Jewish refugees had to have a pass card stamped by General Ghoya. Mom felt lucky on the weeks she was able to get a stamp on her card, seen at right.

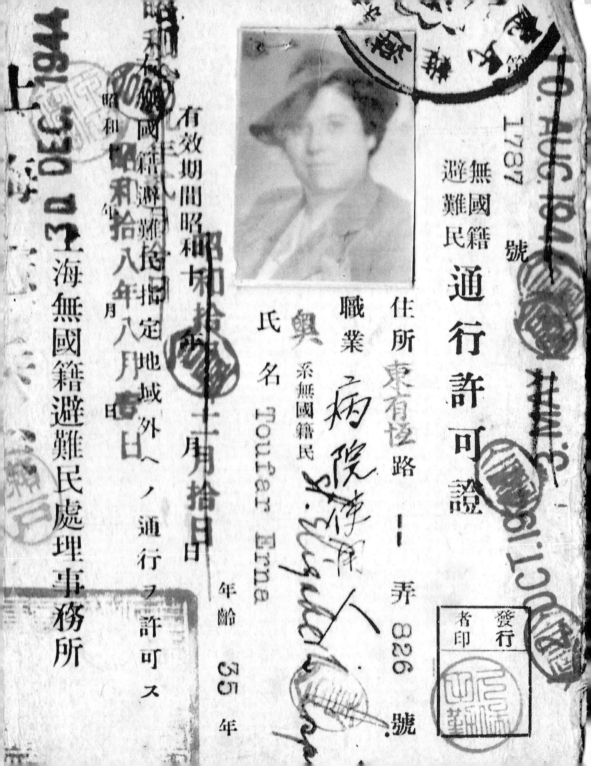

無國籍
避難民
通行許可證

第 1787 號

住所 東有恆路 一 弄 826 號

職業 奥 系無國籍民

氏名 Toufar Erna

病院傳染用人

A. Elisabeth

年齡 35 年

有效期間昭和十
昭和十 二月拾日

昭和 年 月 日

在滬無國籍避難民限拾捌指定地域外ヘノ通行ヲ許可ス

上海無國籍避難民處理事務所

發行
者印

10. AUG. 1944

30 DEC 1944
上海

DCT. 1944

Chapter 14

June, 1943

Though Lily adapted quickly to her new surroundings, some days were tougher than others. A few months after starting at the Kadoorie School, Lily walked into Mr. Meyer's class and sat at her desk. But she did not sit for long.

"Line up to go outside, students," Mr. Meyer ordered as soon as he entered the room. "We're going to run laps around the courtyard."

Lily groaned. She hated this exercise that her teacher insisted upon every week.

"I will make strong athletes out of all of you," Mr. Meyer shouted as he urged his students around the perimeter of the yard.

"Does Mr. Meyer think we're part of the German soccer team?" Lily moaned under her breath. She could not see the benefit of these weekly exercises or the value of sports in general. She was content with a good book or a chance to be with her friends. But she had no choice about having to complete these laps!

Around the courtyard she ran, lap after agonizing lap until, finally, she sank down onto the grass, rolled over onto her back, and gazed up at the clear, blue sky. Wisps of cloud dotted the horizon and a warm breeze swept over her. It was a perfect day, and she could have happily spent the afternoon lying there looking up. Just then, one of the girls in her class jumped over her. It was Daisy.

"Come on," Daisy shouted. "I'll race you around the track."

Lily shook her head. "Just leave me here. I can't walk another step."

Daisy would have none of it. She grabbed Lily by the arm and began to drag her across the grassy courtyard. "If you don't want to run, I'll pull you around."

Lily laughed out loud and allowed herself to be hauled across the field. She was thinking this wasn't such a bad way to be moved when suddenly she slithered over something warm and soft. Daisy came to a stop and froze. When Lily checked, she realized that she had slid across a large mound of dog poop that had been hidden by a tuft of taller grass on the field. She was covered in it from her waist down to her shoes.

Daisy dropped Lily's arm and clapped her hand across her mouth. Her eyes were round and popping from her head. Lily stared in disbelief as well. Just then, Mr. Meyer signalled everyone to get in a line and march back to the classroom. Lily was mortified. She looked down at her brown-streaked clothes and up at Daisy, who had still not moved. What would she do? There was no way Lily would let the other students see her; she would be the laughing stock of the entire class. But what choice did she have? Mr. Meyer was pointing at her now, and motioning for her to line up. Daisy gave her an apologetic shrug, then moved off to join the others. Lily waited a few more seconds before following her.

At first no one seemed to notice. Lily tried to shield the dirty side of her body from her classmates. Perhaps she would be able to sneak into her seat and finish out the day with no one seeing. But that wasn't possible. As she joined the line in the warmth of that beautiful early summer sunshine, a small gust of wind wafted over her and carried with it a disgusting smell.

"Something stinks," one of her classmates shouted. Everyone looked around, wondering where the vile odor was coming from. And finally, all eyes came to rest on Lily.

Her face burned and she quickly lowered her head. But there was no hiding the mess – and certainly not the smell. One by one, the students moved away from her until Lily stood alone in the center of a ring of children who were all staring and holding their noses. Mr. Meyer pretended it was nothing.

"We've all had our own problems in the past," he said. "Move on back to class."

Lily spent the rest of the day sitting in her filthy clothes with her head down, not wanting to look at anyone. Daisy kept apologizing for days after that, though Lily knew it was an accident and didn't want to talk about it. The less said, the better. Thankfully, her classmates did not tease her too much, and, within days, the incident was forgotten by most of them. Most, that is, except Lily.

But if she thought that school day was the worst ever, it was quickly replaced by something even more terrible. This time, it was during Japanese language class. Lily was actually enjoying the new language, as she liked learning all languages. She was good at Russian, French, and English, and she knew she would be good at Japanese, as well. But on this day, she was not paying attention to Mr. Tobias. She was bored by the repetition of verbs and was busy whispering to several of her friends who sat close by.

"Quiet, Miss Toufar," warned Mr. Tobias.

Lily stopped talking, but seconds later resumed her whispered conversation.

"Miss Toufar, I think you had better pay attention." This time Mr. Tobias's voice was louder and more stern.

Lily ignored him again and continued speaking softly with her friends.

"Miss Toufar! This is your last warning!" bellowed her teacher.

But still, Lily would not be quieted. She was busy whispering to her neighbor about the rickshaw ride that she was going to take with her Aunt Nini later that day. She didn't even hear Mr. Tobias approach until she was startled to attention by the gunshot *whack* of his ruler on her desk. Lily jumped and looked up into the face of her teacher.

"I warned you, Miss Toufar. Hands out in front of you!"

Lily could not believe what was about to happen. She had seen other students, mostly boys, receive the ruler across their knuckles. Once, Harry had shown her the red welts on his own hands after he had been walloped for forgetting to bring his homework. There were marks across the back of his hands for days. But never Lily! She had never been punished for anything in the past. That was about to change.

"I'm sorry, Mr. Tobias," Lily pleaded softly. "It won't happen again."

"Too late for apologies, Miss Toufar. I said hands in front of you." Mr. Tobias spoke in a low menacing voice.

You could have heard a pin drop. All eyes were on Lily. She gulped and looked around, searching for a way out of this mess and finding nothing. Finally and slowly, she brought her hands up from her lap where she had clenched them, and held them, palms down and trembling, in front of her teacher. Mr. Tobias planted his feet firmly on the floor and raised the ruler above his head. But just as he began to swing the ruler down onto Lily's knuckles, she swiped her hands out of its path. Mr. Tobias's ruler whipped through the air, past Lily's desk, and landed with a loud *thwack* against his own leg!

Everyone gasped, including Lily. Mr. Tobias's face contorted in agony though he didn't make a sound. After a moment of painful silence, he turned from Lily's desk and walked slowly back to his own. He sat down heavily and closed his eyes. When he finally opened them, he resumed the lesson as if nothing had happened. Lily was never punished for whispering that day, though she made a point of staying out of Mr. Tobias's way from then on…and staying dead quiet in his class.

Chapter 15

November, 1943

Lily would have loved to tell her father the story of how she swiped her hands away from Mr. Tobias's ruler. In times gone by, Pop would probably have laughed out loud as she described the look on her teacher's face. He might even have shared a story or two of his own about how he was once punished in school when he was a boy. They would have laughed together over those memories. But as the weeks and months went by in the Hongkew ghetto, laughter began to disappear from Lily's home along with the opportunity to share stories with Pop. The joy was being sucked out of her parents, leaving them silent and troubled most days. Lily tried to smile in front of them. She wanted to show them that she was young and healthy and could get through anything. But by the time she had lived in the ghetto for six months, even she was beginning to suffer under the difficult conditions there.

Lily was playing in the haystack behind the SACRA one evening. She still had difficulty ignoring the radio tower that loomed over the fence behind the apartment building, along with the knowledge that the Japanese police were watching the Jewish refugees inside the ghetto. Sometimes Lily would almost feel the eyes of the guards peering over the fence at her, her friends, and her family members as they went about their day. She tried to shrug it off, but the twisted knot in her stomach never seemed to disappear when she played there.

"They can watch as much as they like," Harry said, climbing to the top of the haystack and standing up tall with his arms above his head.

"How can you be so sure they won't do anything to us?" Lily asked. She still had nightmares about General Ghoya slapping the face of the Jewish man in the line up ahead of her mother.

Harry shrugged. "Just let them try something with me. I'll stand up to them and show them I'm not scared." He slid down the haystack, shouting at the top of his lungs, and jumped to his feet at the bottom.

Lily wasn't sure anyone could stand up to the Japanese police who guarded the ghetto. She would never convince Harry of that, though. A small mouse ran out from underneath the haystack and staggered across Lily's shoe. It looked sick – almost dead. Without a second thought, Lily bent, picked up the mouse by the tail, and threw it over the back wall. She wiped her hand down her trousers and turned back to Harry. In the months since she had moved into the ghetto, she had become very accustomed to the mice and even the larger rats that roamed the streets, competing with citizens for whatever scraps of food they could find. The biggest thing to fear about these rodents was the disease they carried – disease that could lead to infections like meningitis that caused your brain and spinal cord to swell. People died from that disease. Lily's parents had warned her to never get too close to these pests, but they were so bold. Not even shouting, clapping, or stamping your feet would make them run away.

Harry was about to charge the haystack one last time. "Come on," he shouted. "I'll race you to the top."

Lily thought she was up for the challenge. She sprinted up the haystack next to Harry, trying to shove him aside. But it was no good. The months in the ghetto, and the little food that she had to eat, had sapped her of energy and strength.

"You win," she said, breathless, when she finally reached the top.

Harry was sitting there, victorious. "I'm the strongest one in the ghetto!" he crowed. He may have won this race, but Lily could see that he, too, was struggling to catch his breath.

Just then, Mom appeared at the window of their apartment. She leaned out and shouted, "It's time to come in."

Lily said good-bye to Harry and entered the apartment building.

Even climbing the stairs was becoming difficult, she realized. Her body felt weak, and it was an effort to drag herself up the last flight. She didn't want Mom to see this. So, just before entering her flat, Lily paused, took a deep breath, and pinched her cheeks to bring out the red and make them appear less pale. It seemed to work. Her parents didn't notice anything out of the ordinary.

Supper that night was a small bowl of rice with some beans mixed in. It hardly satisfied the pangs in Lily's stomach, but she didn't say a word. She knew that as hard as everything felt to her, Mom and Pop were suffering so much more. What little food they had was given to her first. Extra blankets were piled on her bed. Pennies were reserved for small treats that came her way. It was hard to complain when her parents had less of everything.

Lily finished up her meal and helped Pop clear the dishes. Then she got ready for bed. She scratched at her arm, absently. Whenever she played outside near the haystack, she always came home with bumps and welts from the mosquitos, gnats, and beetles that lived there and were only too happy to feast on anyone who came near.

"Lily, please don't scratch," Mom warned. "It will become infected."

Lily paused and clenched her teeth. If she counted to ten, the worst part of the itching might subside.

"We'll keep the window closed tonight," Mom continued. "That way, the bugs won't get inside."

Lily knew that wasn't necessarily true. No matter what her parents did, insects always invaded the inside of their apartment. Spiders crawled out of the tiniest cracks in the floorboards, and when Lily went to stomp on them, they would magically disintegrate into a bit of dust. The centipedes were even worse with their hundred tiny legs moving like soldiers on parade. And once a week, Mom would help Lily wash her hair with strong bleach to prevent the spread of lice, which could also lead to deadly diseases such as typhus.

Just before Lily was ready to lie down, Pop lit a candle and ran it along the edge of her mattress, trying to burn the bedbugs that had settled there. It would only help a little. By morning, she would awaken to a fresh set of bites and sores on her arms and legs.

Finally, Lily lay her head down on her pillow. It was cold in the flat and she shivered as she pulled the thin blanket up to her neck. Pop came to sit next to her, breathing heavily as he settled on the mattress. Behind him, Mom's knitting needles clicked softly as her fingers wove complicated patterns into the sweater she was working on. Whenever Mom was not at the convent, or not working on their family finances, she could be found with a ball of yarn and her knitting needles. Lily knew that her mother would be knitting well into the night, long after she and Pop had gone to sleep.

"I gave some food to one of the beggars in front of my store today," said Pop. "He was a Jewish man. I couldn't bear to look at him. His body was stick thin. He wasn't even wearing any shoes – just dirty strips of cloth wrapped around his feet." Pop closed his eyes as if to block out the image. "He said his family had been driven out of their shelter because they had no more money. He actually wanted to give me his shirt in exchange for something to eat."

Every day, Lily saw Chinese men, women, and children who begged for food on the streets. For some reason, it was always harder to hear about a Jew – one of their own – in that same desperate situation. *Pop's eyes look so sad,* thought Lily. The lines that ran across his forehead were deeper and more creased than ever before.

"I'm glad you helped that man."

"It wasn't enough," Pop replied. "It will never be enough." He sighed again, more deeply this time. "How about a story tonight, Lily."

"Oh, yes, please," Lily replied, relieved to stop hearing about the Jewish beggar. "You haven't read to me in such a long time."

Pop smiled weakly and reached for her book of Grimm's fairy tales. The clicking of Mom's knitting needles continued to keep a soft beat in the background, accompanying Pop as he read to Lily, until her eyes began to droop, and she drifted off to sleep.

Chapter 16

Lily could live with the mice and even the bugs. In fact, after several more months in the ghetto, she almost forgot about the itching that, at first, had driven her crazy. She stopped shuddering every time a mouse ran over the tip of her shoe. And she stopped paying attention to the grime in the streets and inside their apartment. But the thing she couldn't adjust to, the one thing that was always on her mind, was hunger. Her stomach felt empty from early morning until bedtime. It was almost like a physical pain that gnawed at her insides. There was so little food to eat in the ghetto.

There was some help in the form of aid that came from an organization called the Jewish Joint Distribution Committee. With funding from the International Red Cross, the JDC had established an office and a soup kitchen in the heart of Hongkew. Jewish refugees lined up for hours to receive one small meal a day. But often, the food that came in was rotting and not even fit for the dogs that roamed the streets, let alone the citizens of the ghetto. Pop's shoe store was struggling along. Money was scarce and the little that Lily's family could pull together was used to buy rice, beans, and a few precious vegetables from the outdoor market. Meat was a rare treat. And during the weeks when Mom was denied the stamp on her pass card, there was even less food on their table. Lily was starving and growing thinner by the day.

She could see the worry growing in her parents' eyes as she left the apartment for school every morning, struggling to look alert and strong. It was getting harder to fool her Mom and Pop, and sometimes even the effort of smiling was too much for Lily.

One Sunday morning in late December, Pop approached Lily to go with him on an outing. "I'm going to try to sell some things in the market," he said. "Come with me, Lily."

This was not the first time Pop had gone to peddle wares in an open field at one end of Hongkew. Once a week, after having already worked more than seventy hours, he would take shoes from his store, and, with Willi, he would go to sell them, trying every way he could to make money for food that his family could eat. Lily lifted her head from her cot where she was resting and stared at her father.

"The fresh air will do you good," he said.

All Lily really wanted to do was to stay curled up in bed on this cold December day. Her body felt so weak and the thought of walking through the ghetto on this outing was almost too much for her. But there was such eagerness in Pop's eyes. She knew it would make him happy if she agreed to go along. "Can Susie come with us?" Lily asked.

Pop nodded. "Of course. We'll pick her up on the way." And that was enough to make Lily rise from her bed, put on her sweater and coat, and join her father at the door.

Before they left, Mom forced a spoonful of cod-liver oil down Lily's throat, as she did every morning before school. "It's good for you," she said. "It will keep you healthy."

Lily wrinkled her nose and squeezed her eyes shut as she opened her mouth to receive the thick fishy-tasting goo. *How can anything so disgusting be good for you*, she wondered, as the oil slid its way down her throat. The cod-liver oil may have been helping to keep Lily healthy, but it was doing nothing to increase her weight. Her ribs stuck out from her chest. Her arms were beginning to look like twigs, and her legs looked as if they couldn't hold her body up. Mom wrapped a wool scarf tightly around Lily's neck and she followed her father out the door.

Today, in addition to the shoes that Pop carried in a sack over his shoulder, he also carried pots and dishes from their home. "What good are pots and pans when there is nothing to cook?" Pop said when Lily questioned him about his bundle. "May as well sell them and get a few more cents." He shifted the weight to his other shoulder, bending from the load. Pop was losing weight, too. His pants were loose and drooping around his waist, and he had pounded extra holes in his leather belt to hold them in place. He had always looked so strong to Lily. Now he was thin and as wiry as some of the Chinese men that Lily saw pushing carts around the ghetto.

As promised, Lily and her father stopped by Susie's apartment on their way to the field. Susie was happy to join her friend on the outing, and the two girls set off after Pop. Lily pulled her wool scarf up over her head and shivered. She had become so thin that it was hard to stay

Some days, Pop would take shoes and other wares to sell in the market stalls on Yuhang Road.

warm, even with the extra layers of clothing that Mom had piled on her. Susie shuddered next to her and Lily glanced over at her friend.

"Are you okay?" she asked.

"Cold," Susie replied.

Perhaps they would warm up once they reached the field where merchants had gathered to sell their wares in the open market. The space was already packed when Pop, Lily, and Susie arrived. Pop quickly staked out a small space in the middle of the field and spread a blanket on the ground in front of him. The shoes he had carried in one of the large bundles were placed in rows on one side of the blanket. On the other side, he began to arrange the pots, pans, and dishes he had brought from their apartment. Lily and Susie helped, and before long, everything was in place.

Within minutes, Pop had grabbed the attention of a woman who was wandering through the market. "Can I interest you in a pair of good boots?" he asked, spreading his arms wide and inviting the woman to take a look at his samples. "With this colder weather, everyone needs boots, and you won't find finer ones anywhere in the ghetto." The woman looked interested and Pop sensed that he might have his first sale of the day.

Lily watched in awe, admiring her father's expert skill as a salesman, not to mention his charm. But before long, she grew tired of standing in the market and as the temperature dropped, shivers began rippling up and down her body.

"I'm bored," whispered Susie. "And still freezing!"

Lily nodded. "Pop, Susie and I are going for a walk."

Pop looked up and waved in Lily's direction. "Fine, fine. Don't be too long," he said and returned to negotiating with his client.

Lily and Susie set out to explore the market. But there was little of interest here for them; just broken and used housewares for sale along with old clothes that smelled. There weren't even any interesting books. Before long, they had left the market and were wandering in the streets behind the open field. No one paid any attention to the two young girls who were roaming the ghetto, unsupervised.

"This isn't helping," Susie said, hopping from foot to foot trying to warm up. "I can't feel my toes."

"Maybe it wasn't such a good idea to come out with Pop, today," Lily said, longing for the bed she had left behind that morning. Just then, she spotted a large canvas tent that was behind the field. It looked almost like the kind of circus tent she had once seen in Vienna, years earlier. "Let's go in there. Maybe it'll be warm inside."

Susie hesitated, but Lily grabbed her by the hand and dragged her through the flap doors of the tent. It took a moment for Lily's eyes to adjust to the dim light inside. She and Susie stood at the entrance, squinting at ghostly images that slowly emerged from murky shadows. Lily felt Susie's hand tightening on her arm.

The tent was filled with old Chinese men, squatting or lying on the ground. Some of them were sleeping. Most were smoking long pipes. A hazy cloud hung in the air. *It is definitely warm in here,* thought Lily. *In fact, it's almost stifling.* The pipe fumes were too much for her. Smoke traveled up her nose and into her lungs. She and Susie coughed and gagged.

"I don't want to be in here." Susie choked the words out.

They turned and ran from the tent, gasping for air. The old men barely looked up. Once outside, Susie had had enough. "I'm going home," she said. "Sorry, Lily, but this is no fun." And with that, she turned and walked away, leaving Lily alone on the streets of Hongkew. *This day is going downhill fast,* Lily thought. She couldn't blame Susie for deserting her. She longed to go home as well. But first she returned to the market to find Pop. She found him in a good mood.

"I'm making some sales," he said, when Lily told him that she wanted to leave. "I can't go yet."

Lily stood helplessly watching as an elderly woman bartered with her father for a couple of pots. By now, the cold had reached into Lily's jacket and through her arms and legs. The hollowness in her stomach only added to the spasms that shook her body. How long would she have to wait for Pop? At that moment Pop looked up and met Lily's pleading eyes. He sighed. "You go home, Lily."

"I'm s…s…sorry, Pop." Lily stuttered the words out. "I guess I sh…shouldn't have come, today."

"No, it's my fault. I don't want you getting sick. But here," he added, reaching into his pocket. "Take this money and buy some milk on the way home." He placed a few precious coins into her outstretched hand, and with that, he returned to his sales. Lily walked back onto the street. She didn't mind having this time alone, and after so many months of living in Hongkew, Lily could navigate her way around the ghetto with ease. Holding the few cents that Pop had given her, she set out for home.

There was no refrigerator in their apartment and nowhere to keep fresh produce for more than a day or two. This was hardly a problem since the family rarely had leftover food to keep. Mom usually bought milk in thimble-sized containers that could be finished quickly, before it went bad. On this day, Lily entered the small provision store and looked around. The shelves were almost empty. The shopkeeper, an elderly Jewish man, barely looked up from his newspaper. Lily headed to the back of the store and the small icebox that held the cartons of milk. She paid for six small containers, counting the money carefully before handing it over to the shop owner. He grunted his thanks before Lily headed out the door toward home.

The little containers of milk were in a paper bag that Lily held close to her chest. *No one is going to grab my precious milk,* she thought. As she walked, she wondered what the coming winter months in the ghetto would be like. Winter back in Frenchtown had been harsh. But Lily worried that here, where the building walls were paper thin and there was no heating whatsoever, the winter would be brutal.

The milk containers bounced up and down inside the brown

paper bag. Lily's stomach was growling more than usual, and without thinking, she reached into the bag, pulled out one of the little cartons, popped open the lid, and drank the milk down in one quick gulp. It was delicious, and, for a moment, Lily closed her eyes and allowed herself to enjoy the creamy flavor. There were five containers left in the bag. *Mom will never notice*, Lily thought.

On she walked, past the big jail that was on Ward Street. Inside were mostly Chinese prisoners. Lily wondered if they got any food at all during their long days of confinement. She reached into the bag again, pulled out another small carton, and after just a moment's hesitation, she opened the lid and drank that one, too. Two of the six were now gone. What excuse was Lily going to give her mother? She couldn't say that the milk had been stolen. Why would a thief make off with only two tiny containers? *Will Mom believe me if I say I dropped them? Probably not.*

The walk home was beginning to warm Lily's body. And the taste of the sweet milk was on her lips. It was so good, and her stomach cried out for just a little bit more. And although she warned herself to stop now, there was just no controlling the longing that overtook her. Lily reached into the bag one last time and quickly drank two more containers of milk. With only two remaining, Lily climbed the stairs to her apartment and faced her mother.

Mom looked inside the bag and then stared at Lily who stood with her head down ready to receive whatever punishment Mom doled out. *It'll be worth it*, Lily thought. Her stomach felt almost normal for the first time in weeks. Finally, Mom closed the bag and sighed deeply.

"Go and get ready for bed, Lily," she said.

Lily looked up in disbelief. "But what about the milk?" she asked.

Mom shook her head. "I think you need it more than any of us. I wish there was more to give."

Lily was spared, and neither her mother nor her father mentioned anything about the milk. But as wonderful as the taste of that creamy liquid had been, it had only filled her stomach for a moment. Soon she was just as hungry as before, and she could only dream about one day having all the milk she could manage to drink.

Chapter 17

Some weeks later, Mom came home from work with a special treat; one that she knew would help ease the hunger that overwhelmed Lily. Using their precious savings, Mom had bought a large piece of meat from the convent kitchen. It was a beef tongue, a delicacy that Lily had not eaten in many months. Mom promised that she would boil it with some vegetables and serve up a feast for the family. In fact, the whole family – Lily's aunts and uncles – had been invited to share in the spread.

Lily couldn't contain her excitement. The family hadn't gathered together for a meal since moving into the ghetto. Lily missed those dinners and family conversations that drifted around the table. She even missed her Uncle Willi teasing her with his stories. These days, Uncle Willi had other things on his mind and had little time for his young niece. Not only was he working long hours with Pop in the shoe store, but Willi had met a girl, and what little spare time he had was spent with her. Her name, like Lily's best friend, was Susi, and Lily thought she was beautiful. She had thick, dark curly hair, full round lips, and almond-shaped eyes. Lily wondered if Uncle Willi was going to marry this Susi and secretly hoped that she would soon have a new aunt.

That evening, Willi was accompanied to Lily's apartment by his little dog, Meckie. Lily was delighted to meet this latest member of the family. "He's so cute," she said, dropping to her knees and hugging the little white terrier. The dog was small and friendly, not like the giant dogs that her former neighbor, Mrs. Kinecky, had owned in Frenchtown. Meckie wagged his tail and reached up to lick Lily on the cheek. They were instant friends. "Where did you get him?"

Willi shrugged. "Nowhere, really. I came out of the shoe store one day, and there he was. He followed me home and he's been with me ever since." Most

Lily often played with Willi's dog, Meckie.

149

days, Meckie just wandered the streets of Hongkew with the other dogs that roamed loose in the ghetto. But Willi said that he always returned to him in the evening.

Lily played with Meckie in a corner of the apartment until Mom called her to help put the finishing touches on the evening meal. The tongue was simmering in a pot of boiling water that rested on the small electric burner close to the window. Lily's job was to go through the bag of white rice that Mom had dumped in the center of the table, and pick out the beetles and other insects that might have nested there. Sometimes these bags of rice teamed with bugs. Today, there were just a few, and Lily quickly squished them between her fingers. *That was easy*, she thought. It was so much worse when she found worms in the flour that her mother used for baking. They were uglier than the bugs and popped between her fingers. Next, Lily had to wash the vegetables that were going to go in the pot with the meat. Lily had learned never to drink the water in the ghetto. Everyone was afraid of dysentery, an illness where your stomach swelled and you suffered with severe cramps and terrible diarrhea. The poisonous bacteria that lead to this disease bred in the water that flowed from the pipes of Hongkew. Untreated, it was enough to kill small children and make even the strongest adult sick for weeks. The water that Lily's parents brought into the apartment had to be boiled and treated with a few drops of peroxide, a kind of bleach that killed the bacteria. Mom brought the precious drops home from the convent. Nothing, not even wilting vegetables, could come in contact with water that had not first been treated with the chemical.

Once Lily had cleaned the vegetables and they had been added to the pot, she went back to the corner of the apartment to play with Meckie. The smell coming from the simmering meat was heavenly. All her aunts and uncles *oohed* and *aahed* over the meal that was about to be served.

"When will it be time?" Pop asked. "If it isn't ready soon, I swear I will reach into that pot and eat the meat raw!"

Everyone laughed, including Lily. For one evening, she could forget about bugs and rats and dirt and just enjoy being together with her parents and relatives, sharing a meal and some much-needed laughter. Lily vowed that she would try to think less about her stomach and more about how grateful she was for her family. *Maybe Pop is right,* thought Lily, as she glanced around the room. He had always said that as long as the family was together, everything would be okay. The aroma coming from the bubbling pot was becoming intoxicating. She inhaled over and over, as if the smell alone could fill her up.

Finally, everyone gathered around the table. It was minutes now until the meal was ready. But just as Lily was about to sit down, there was a loud shriek behind her. She whirled around in time to see a large stray cat that had entered the room through the open window. Drawn by the smell of meat, the cat had climbed up to their apartment, and, while no one was paying attention, it had dipped its paw into the pot of boiling water, grabbed the entire piece of meat, and was about to run back out the window and disappear into the streets, their dinner firmly clenched between its teeth. But not if her mother had anything to say about it.

"You wicked, wicked animal!" screamed Mom. "Get back here before I slice you in half and boil you as well."

Mom lunged for the cat, which quickly disappeared out the window. She turned and flew out the door, down the stairs, in hot pursuit of the cat. For a moment, no one moved. Then the entire family ran out the door onto the street. They could see Mom weaving this way and that, around rickshaws and little carts, pushing children and old women out of her way as she stayed just within an arm's grasp of the cat that had stolen their dinner.

People on the street stopped in their tracks, watching this crazed woman tear down the road shouting at the top of her lungs for the thief to stop. Suddenly, Mom vanished around a corner, leaving her family members standing in disbelief with their mouths open. Slowly and silently, they turned and trudged back up the stairs of the building and into the apartment. Lily was worried about her mother who had disappeared from view, but she was horrified that their dinner might be gone.

"If anyone can catch that cat, your mother can," Pop said weakly. "And if not, well then, we'll just have to make do with a smaller meal."

Lily sank to the floor next to Meckie and eyed the little dog.

"What happened to you?" she whispered under her breath. "Why didn't you protect us and our supper?" Meckie yawned and rolled over to have his belly scratched. Lily folded her arms across her chest and stared into space.

Minutes went by, and finally, there was the sound of footsteps on the stairs. Lily leapt to her feet and ran for the door of the apartment. She flung it open and there was Mom. Even though it was freezing outside, sweat streamed down her face. Her hair was stuck in clumps on her forehead, and her apron was stained and ripped across the bottom. But worst of all, Mom's hands hung down by her side – empty! Pop pushed past Lily and pulled Mom into the apartment, guiding her to a chair at the table. Everyone waited for her to speak.

"I almost had that little thief," Mom finally whispered, staring down at her hands. "I had the tip of his tail in my fingers, but he managed to pull away. I just couldn't run anymore."

"Don't worry, Erna," Pop replied. "You tried your best. We'll be fine with what we have, isn't that right, everyone?"

Lily's aunts and uncles murmured their agreement while Lily stood apart from her family, staring in disbelief. She did not feel fine about their lost dinner. She was angry and disappointed, and above all, hungry! But what could she say? She only had to look at her mother's dishevelled appearance to know that Mom had tried everything in her power to get their meal back.

Slowly and quietly, the family assembled at the table and took their seats. They passed around small platters of boiled vegetables and bowls of rice. Just before eating, Pop stood and faced his family.

"I know this isn't the meal that any of us expected, tonight," he began, his eyes on Lily. She felt her cheeks burn as Pop continued. "We don't know how long we will remain imprisoned in this ghetto. And we don't really know where the next good meal will come from. But we're together as a family. And that's what is most important." Pop sank back down into his chair as the family began to eat.

Pop told the story of how the cat had stolen their dinner every night for weeks after that. The story became so embellished and exaggerated that it was hard to know what was true and what wasn't. Lily would laugh uncontrollably whenever her father told the tale. After a while, she almost forgot how hungry and disappointed she had been that evening.

Chapter 18

February, 1944

The winter months that followed were just as harsh as Lily had feared they would be. Nothing could warm her as the cold air snuck into their apartment and settled there like an unwanted tenant. Her parents didn't seem to mind the icy temperatures. Pop would clap his arms around his body, put on his jacket, and head out for the shoe store.

"The cold keeps me awake during the long days," he would say. "It's so much better than the unbearable heat in summer."

Mom was just as accepting of the cold. She had also found the heat oppressive. But not Lily. At night, she huddled under several blankets trying desperately to stop the shivers that rattled her thin body. Daytimes were just as bad. Even with layers of sweaters and jackets, Lily could not stay warm. She prayed every day for the cold and dampness of winter to leave. But winter seemed to drag on endlessly.

One morning, Lily lay on her bed, listening to Mom move about the room. Any minute now, Mom would tell her to get up and get ready for school. But Lily wasn't quite ready to face the day. She burrowed underneath her blankets trying to let sleep reclaim her for just a few more minutes. Sleep was the only place where she didn't feel chilled and she longed to go back there and dream about the warm sun on her face. It wasn't going to happen. The cold was seeping through the covers, and she needed to get dressed while she had any warmth left in her body. Taking a deep breath, Lily threw back her blankets and lunged for her clothes, grabbing her thickest sweater and warmest wool socks. She was leaning over a small bowl to splash water on her face when Mom spoke.

"Lily, come home quickly after school today. There's a new café on Chusan Road. I thought we could go together this afternoon."

Lily paused, shivering from the ice-cold water. "What's the occasion, Mom?"

"It's been almost a year since we moved into the ghetto. And so far, we're still healthy and together. You're doing well in school, and your father and I are working and trying to save a bit of money. I thought that was worth a little celebration."

A whole year! Lily reeled from the realization. How much longer would they have to stay in Hongkew?

The Kadoorie School was just as cold as her apartment building. Lily's fingers cramped as she moved her pencil across the page.

Strangely, running around the courtyard that day with Mr. Meyer was the only way that Lily felt any warmth at all. Blood began to pulse in her legs and she could feel the sweat roll from her forehead. But the warm glow after that exercise didn't last. The cold found a way to burrow back into Lily's body, leaving her shivering once more. The only thing she was looking forward to was the outing with Mom, and she rushed home after school so that they could set out together.

In spite of the fact that there was so little food in the ghetto, somehow the Jews of Hongkew were managing to open shops and restaurants. The restaurants were not nearly as grand as the ones that had been established in the French Concession, and there was not always very much on the menu. Owners improvised with scarce ingredients to create a few treats. But these small restaurants certainly helped lift the spirits of the Jews who were living in the designated area. This one was called the Roof Garden Café. It had pale pink walls and floral curtains. Soft music played in the background. Lily and her mother sat at a little round table and ordered tea and a small, sweet tart to share.

Mom handed over a few precious coins to the owner and smiled at her daughter. "It's worth it," she said. "If I close my eyes, I can picture Vienna how it used to be. Cafés like this one were everywhere in the city."

Lily closed her eyes. She had few memories of a life before their move to Shanghai. Even Frenchtown was a distant dream for Lily. But for the moment, it didn't matter. She wrapped her fingers around the hot cup of tea and took a sip. Warm liquid traveled down her throat, warming her insides. And when she bit into the pastry crust and tasted the sweet jam that oozed from the center, she felt content, as if life was normal. She looked up at her mother.

"Do you think we'll ever leave here, Mom?" she asked. The family rarely spoke of the future and Lily had never asked this question before.

Mom paused, her teacup suspended in the air between the saucer and her lips. Then she set it down with a light rattle. "I pray every day that all of this will end, and we'll be able to leave," she said somberly. Lily didn't reply. "But we're managing, aren't we, my darling?" Lily nodded. She didn't trust herself to speak. Finally Mom sighed and raised her teacup once more. "What would you want if we weren't here?"

Lily didn't know how to answer that question. She didn't know what she longed for. This was the only life she could remember. What did she really know of toys or presents or new clothes? Finally she stammered a reply. "Nothing, I guess, except maybe to be warm in the winter." It was such a simple wish.

Mom leaned forward and stared into Lily's eyes. "One day, I pray we will live in a place where you are warm in the winter, Lily."

Eventually, the winter did pass and by early April, Lily had pushed the harshness of those bitter cold months to the back of her mind. *I won't have to worry about winter for months*, she thought. *And maybe by then, Mom's prayers for a warm place will come true.*

On Friday, April 7, the family celebrated the first night of Passover. They had been invited over to a family friend's for the Seder, the dinner that marked the beginning of the festival. But before that, they were all going to go to the synagogue. The Ohel Moshe Synagogue was on Ward Street just down the road from the prison. Though her family did not go to the synagogue often, Lily was always impressed when she entered the main sanctuary. It wasn't large, and the wooden pews where the Jews sat were simple and unadorned. But the altar that held the Torah scrolls at the front of the room was covered in a thick, red-velvet curtain with large white Stars of David embroidered across them. The curtains and the scrolls likely came from Europe before the war. Here, in the Hongkew synagogue, they were a reminder of the religious life that Jews had left behind.

Lily and her mother climbed to the second floor of the building, a section that was reserved for women. The men worshipped below them. Lily peered over the railing and sought out her father, sitting in the third row next to Willi, Walter, and Poldi. Pop turned around and looked up, as if he could sense his daughter's eyes on him. He smiled ever so slightly and then turned back to his prayers. Rabbi Ashkenazi was leading the congregation in song. His voice rose and fell with a brilliant vibrato that echoed in the hall. Everyone joined in to respond to the verses. Lily knew the tunes, having learned many of them at the after-school Hebrew lessons that she attended here at the synagogue. She sang in a strong clear voice.

After the service, the family went to the apartment of Mr. and Mrs. Cohen. The Cohens had known Lily's family back in Vienna before the war. At first, when Lily heard that they were being invited to someone's home for Passover, she had been excited. They rarely went out to other people's homes. But as soon as Lily walked through the doors of the Cohen family's apartment, her enthusiasm faded. She was the only child there that evening, and Mr. and Mrs. Cohen were observant Jews. They attended synagogue regularly and followed the customs and rules of the Jewish religion as thoroughly as they could. There would be a long set of prayers and readings before the Seder meal would be served, and by now, Lily was starving. She looked longingly at her mother whose eyes warned her to be still. She slumped in her seat and rested her head on her hand.

The readings began, and, before long, Lily was completely bored. It was agonizing to sit here and listen to Mr. Cohen ramble through the long passages, thumping his hand on the table for effect. Lily longed for food and pressed her hand against her stomach to quiet the gurgling that erupted from inside her. At one point, when she yawned loudly, Pop threw a stern look in her direction, and she sat up once more in an effort to stay alert. By the time the meal was served, Lily

Lily and the other Jewish families attended the Ohel Moshe Synagogue. Today the synagogue is a museum. The tapestry on the altar is embroidered with the following message: Tribute to the Hongkew People who Provided Refuge to Jews in Time of Need.

was ravenous. There wasn't much on the table, and Lily gulped her soup in three spoonfuls. Everyone had brought a little something to contribute to the meal. There was just enough so that Lily was content.

When dinner was finished, the prayers and singing resumed. Lily, her belly full, could feel her head start to roll and her eyes begin to close. Suddenly, she heard her name, and that brought her back to attention.

Mrs. Cohen was talking and pointing to her. "The youngest one needs to open the door for Elijah."

It was a custom at the Passover Seder to fill a cup of wine and place it in front of an empty chair at the table for the prophet Elijah, who would come as a bearer of peace. But the thought of having to open the door for a ghostly figure to enter the room was terrifying to Lily. She had not thought about Uncle Willi's ghost stories in a long time. But suddenly here she was, confronted with the possibility of a phantom prophet swooping down on her. She shrank down in her seat, suddenly wide awake.

"Lily, I think Mrs. Cohen is asking for your help." Mom nudged Lily to get up.

Lily didn't move. Maybe if she waited long enough, Mrs. Cohen would get someone else to open the door. But no such luck. This time Pop prodded her. "Lily, go and open the door." As he spoke, he pulled Lily's chair out from behind her. She stood, turned around, and walked toward the door of the Cohen apartment. Why did ghostly images always upset her so much? She tried to control her trembling hands and legs, all the while telling herself that she could manage this.

Lily arrived at the door and turned the handle. With a deep breath, she swung the door open. She wanted to turn and run for the safety of her chair. But as scared as she was, Lily stayed at the apartment door, peering down the dark and empty hallway to see if anything was waiting to follow her inside. Nothing appeared, and eventually Lily returned to the table.

The door remained open while everyone continued to sing and pray. Lily's eyes were on the glass of wine, placed in front of the empty chair. She watched the level of the wine for the rest of the night, checking to see if someone or something had taken a sip.

Chapter 19

July, 1944

The whole time Lily and her family were coping with daily hardships in the ghetto, they were also trying to keep up with news of the war in North America, Europe, and countries in the Pacific Ocean. Though the newspapers in Hongkew published daily reports of the conflict around the world, the main source of information came from their shortwave radio. It pulled in news reports from Great Britain and America. But receiving that information was now proving to be difficult. A new proclamation making it illegal for Jewish refugees to own radios had been issued in Hongkew. Pop was fuming the day he slammed the paper on the table and pointed to the announcement that was signed by the Commander-in-Chief of the Japanese Forces in China. It read:

Those who have violated the provisions of this Proclamation or benefited the enemy of Japan shall have their receiving sets confiscated and be severely punished according to military regulations.[4]

"Who do the Japanese think they are, forbidding us to listen to the news?" Pop ranted. At one point, he stuck his head out the small window and bellowed back to where the Japanese soldiers were stationed on the other side of the wall. "You may be able to keep us in here, but you can't stop me from finding out what's going on!" Mom had to pull him back inside and quiet him.

But there was no way, even under threat of punishment, that Pop was going to turn in his radio. In spite of the order, the radio was on as much as possible, bringing in snippets of information about what was happening around the world. And the news was hopeful. In the early hours of June 6, 1944, Lily learned that American, British, and Canadian forces had captured a Nazi stronghold on a beach at Normandy in northern France. In strikes that came from the air and the sea, the German defences had been shattered. The day was being called D-Day, and with it, the news reports were predicting an end to Nazi Germany's rule.

Pop's eyes glowed as he listened to General Eisenhower of the U.S. army announce, *"We will accept nothing less than full victory."*[5]

"It's happening, Lily," Pop said. "We can only pray that the war will end soon."

Lily wanted to believe that the troubles around the world were coming to an end. But she was puzzled about what this would mean to her life here in the ghetto. If the war was reaching its peak in Europe, and Nazi Germany was faltering, would Japan collapse as well? And would that mean that the Jews of Shanghai would be freed from their imprisonment in Hongkew? Was it too much to hope for?

Not all the news they heard was good. The defeat of the Nazis in Normandy was also accompanied by the news that more than nine thousand British, American, and Canadian soldiers had been killed there. It was an overwhelming loss of life, and everyone in Lily's family talked about the brave soldiers who had given their lives for the freedom of others. But in July, the radio announcers began to talk about a new and unimaginable tragedy that was emerging in Europe. Russian troops had marched in and liberated one of the concentration camps that her parents had told her about. This place was called Majdanek. Mom and Pop listened in disbelief when they heard the estimates that more than three hundred and fifty thousand Jews had been murdered there.

"How is that possible?" Mom whispered.

"And that's only one camp. Apparently there were dozens like that one throughout Europe." Pop was beginning to do the math, and the numbers were staggering. "There could be millions dead."

"Our friends?" Mom asked. "The ones who couldn't get out?"

Pop hung his head and said nothing.

Lily listened to the radio and her parents. She couldn't imagine that millions of Jewish people might have been killed in these terrible places. And yet, that's what Pop was saying. After that, her parents were glued to the radio even more than before. When they weren't listening to news reports, they were discussing them with each other and with the other members of the family.

No one imagined what effect all of this was having on Lily. She began to picture thousands of children her age, separated from their parents in concentration camps, and being tortured or killed. Her dreams were filled with mutilated babies and crying mothers. She awoke in a sweat, shoving her pillow into her mouth so that her parents would not hear her cry out. And then, one morning as Lily watched her mother go off to work, she was gripped with a kind of terror that she had not felt before – not when they had moved to Hongkew, not when she was almost hit with Mr. Tobias's ruler, not even when she had watched her mother line up in front of that evil General Ghoya to get her pass card stamped. Lily was suddenly terrified that her mother would be stopped on her way to the convent, maybe even arrested, and Lily would never see her again.

Lily rushed home from school that day and stood by the window of their flat, waiting, worrying, standing on her tiptoes to peer down the road until she finally caught a glimpse of Mom walking up East Yuhang Road toward the SACRA. At the sight of Mom, Lily let out her breath and pressed her hands up to her red-hot cheeks. Still, she said nothing to her parents about how she was feeling.

This continued for several days. Lily tossed and turned through bad dreams each night, and agonized about her parents' safety every day. Then, one night, Pop pulled a book from Lily's shelf and read her the story of Bambi. When Pop got to the part where the young deer's mother was killed, Lily began sobbing uncontrollably.

"My darling child, what is it?" Pop asked. At first Lily couldn't even answer. "Is it the story?"

Lily nodded, trying to catch her breath. It was as if all of the months of living in the ghetto, along with the heat and cold, the dirt, hunger, and disease were coming together in this moment of hopelessness. "Why…why did the mother have to die?" she finally blurted.

"Lily, it's just a fairy tale, that's all." After another minute, Pop sat up on Lily's bed and asked, "Do you think it has something to do with us? Is that why you're crying?"

That brought on a fresh outpouring of tears. How could Lily even begin to explain to her father that she was consumed with worry about Mom and him? In her mind, all she could think about was the possibility that they might be pulled apart, that Mom might be taken from her, or that someone in her family might be killed, just like the Jews in all those concentration camps.

"Lily, please stop crying," Pop pleaded. "You mustn't worry like this."

"I…I don't want you to die, too." Lily's reply was barely a whisper.

Pop cupped Lily's face in his hands and looked into her eyes. "Now, listen to me," he said. "I'm not going to die, and neither is Mom or Willi or Susie, or any or your aunts and uncles. Do you hear what I'm saying to you?"

How can Pop be so sure of that? Lily stared back at her father and nodded slowly.

It took hours for Pop to calm her. That night, Lily still had night-mares about the people she loved dying. It felt as if Pop's promise that the family would stay together was evaporating.

Soon, Lily's fears began to feel even more real. Over the next few months, the Japanese army intensified its presence on the streets of Hongkew. Now the soldiers marched in groups down the main road pointing their rifles in the direction of the citizens of the ghetto. Their faces were angry and hard, and Lily was terrified when she saw them. Pop tried to reason with her.

"It could be a good sign," he said. "The Japanese forces are nervous about the news that the Nazi army is collapsing. The United States is gaining on Japan in the Philippines and Guam, and defeating them in battles close to here. The soldiers in the ghetto are just flexing their muscles a bit to show us they're still in charge, when really, they may be losing their control. It's nothing to worry about, Lily."

Can that be it? wondered Lily. She wasn't sure. She kept her head down when she walked by the Japanese police. She stopped playing in the haystack next to the wall where the Japanese army was posted. Then one day, when she was walking with Mom to meet Pop at the shoe store, she had the most terrifying encounter with the Japanese that she'd had yet.

It was a cloudy day that held the promise of rain. The skies were dark and threatening, and the wind whipped the garbage on the streets up into Lily's face. But that day, she didn't care about the gloomy weather, or the warning signs of rain. Lily was walking next to her mother, holding on to her arm, and telling her about her day at school. She had done very well on a geometry test, and Mr. Gassenheimer had announced her high marks to the class. Mom was delighted with her daughter, and Lily was so excited to tell her Pop how well she'd done at school that she didn't notice the Japanese soldier until she and Mom practically ran into him.

"Papers!" The man barred their way and grunted his command in a low, guttural voice.

Lily shrank away and tried to hide behind her mother. It was common practice for these Japanese guards to stop Chinese citizens of the ghetto and demand to see their identification papers. Lily had witnessed old Chinese men and women being beaten if they didn't respond quickly enough to a soldier's orders. But now the soldiers were beginning to stop Jewish refugees as well. This was new. Lily watched the young soldier who stood in front of them. He wasn't much older than her friend Harry. But this boy had been given great power over the citizens of Hongkew, and they were helpless in the face of his authority.

Mom opened her purse to look for her papers, all the while talking out loud. "I know I put them in here this morning," she said.

Once again, Lily marveled at how calm her mother sounded. She, on the other hand, could feel the sweat gathering at the back of her neck.

"Papers, now!" the young man demanded. His lips pressed into a tight line and he moved one step closer to Mom and Lily.

"Yes, yes," Mom continued, keeping her voice even. "No need to get upset."

This wasn't good. If Mom couldn't produce her papers, what would happen? Would they be arrested? Beaten? In spite of Mom's calmness, Lily could see that the soldier was becoming increasingly angry. He moved even closer until he was practically on top of them.

"I'm just checking this pocket here." Mom still fumbled in her purse, searching for the papers.

The soldier had had enough. Without warning, he suddenly drew back his hand and slapped Mom hard across the face. She staggered backward and Lily let out a scream. Mom quickly brought her hand up to her cheek, but when she moved her hand away, there was a small line of blood oozing across her lower lip. For a moment, no one moved. And then Mom turned to Lily and screamed, "Run, Lily! Get home – now!"

Lily turned on her heel and darted through the growing crowd of people who had gathered to watch the exchange. But after running a few meters, she stopped and turned around, knowing there was no way she could leave her mother. As terrified as she was, she had to stay and see what was going to happen. A short distance from where the Japanese soldier was cross-examining Mom, Lily hid behind a tall pole, peeking her head out to watch the interrogation. From a distance, she could see the blood on Mom's lip trailing down her chin. The soldier towered above her mother, shouting as she continued to rummage frantically through her purse.

Find the paper! Please find it, Lily prayed, helpless to do anything. She stood, shaking, behind the pole, holding her clenched fists up against her mouth to stop herself from crying out.

After what seemed like an eternity, Mom finally pulled her identification document from her purse and thrust it at the soldier. He barely even looked at it before throwing it back at Mom. A moment later, he turned and marched away. Mom stood alone, breathing deeply, before replacing the document in her purse and beginning to walk toward home. When she reached the pole, Lily stepped out from behind her hiding spot. Mom did not say a word. She took Lily's hand and the two of them began to walk toward the SACRA. The rain that had threatened all day began to fall in fat drops that exploded on the pavement. Still, Lily and her Mom walked in deliberate silence through alleys and down narrow lanes, around children squatting in the streets and old men smoking on the corners. When they finally reached the SACRA, they slowly walked up the stairs, into the apartment, and closed the door behind them.

Lily sank to the floor and buried her face in her hands. Only then, did she realize what had just happened, and how close she had come to losing her mother, possibly forever. Could she have done more? Should she have stayed by her mother's side to face whatever punishment the soldier was going to dole out? As relieved as she was that her mother was safe, Lily believed she had deserted Mom at the most dangerous moment of that confrontation. Tears flowed from Lily's eyes, joining the downpour she could hear coming from outside. She stayed on the floor, crying and rocking back and forth until Mom finally took her by the shoulders and pulled her to her feet. Lily buried herself in her mother's arms.

"I'm fine, Lily. I found those silly papers, and he let me go." Mom's voice was still remarkably calm and soothing.

"I'm sorry," Lily wailed. "I never should have run away."

"What are you talking about?" Mom demanded, peeling Lily from her arms and bending to stare into her eyes. "I *told* you to run. You shouldn't have watched. You should have gone straight home."

Lily stared at her mother and struggled to catch her breath. Mom's hair was messy and wet from the rain. The spot on her lip where the blood had appeared was beginning to harden into a dark, ugly bump. Her cheek was red and swollen.

"What do you think you could have done?" Mom continued. "Beaten the soldier back? Even if it were possible, that would have been foolish. You did exactly what I told you to do. You got out of there."

Lily couldn't speak. She was still wracked with guilt for leaving her mother to face the soldier alone. Memories of causing her grand-mother to fall in the apartment swept over her. Even though it made little sense, Lily felt responsible for her mother's wounds, just as she had felt responsible for Oma's injuries and subsequent death.

Mom reached up to touch her swollen lip. "This will heal," she said. "The important thing is that we are both safe."

Over the next few days, the marks on Mom's face went from angry red to deep blue and green. She wore the bruises proudly, telling everyone that she had stood up to the Japanese soldier, though she did make a point of checking to make sure her papers were easily available in her purse before leaving the apartment. Lily was more shaken than ever and more anxious when her mother left for work each morning. Pop had said that the Japanese soldiers were losing their power. To Lily, it felt as if they were becoming a bigger threat.

Chapter 20

It took several days before Lily could talk with Susie about her clash with the Japanese police. The whole incident had shaken her so much, she didn't want to think about it, let alone relive it! Mom's bruises were reminder enough. But eventually, Lily sought out her friend.

"They're monsters," said Susie, listening wide-eyed to Lily's account. "I saw a Japanese soldier kick an old man who was lying on the sidewalk in front of his apartment building. He wasn't doing anything; just sleeping. You're lucky you weren't beaten as well!"

"Pop says their army is getting weaker, but I don't know if I believe him."

The two girls were winding their way down the street toward the Kadoorie School. The rain, which had begun a couple of days earlier, had turned into a torrential downpour causing the streets to flood.

People were calling it a typhoon. The rainwater had mostly receded from East Yuhang Road, but the runoff had brought additional problems. Drains and gutters were backed up and were overflowing with sewage. Lily and Susie jumped over puddles where fleas and mosquitos had found an ideal playground. These stagnant pools would become a breeding ground of infection and disease. The smell on the streets, which on the best of days was overwhelming, was enough to make the two girls gag.

"We heard that the American army captured the Mariana Islands from the Japanese, and they've been bombing Bangkok, too," continued Susie. Her family had also held on to their shortwave radio, despite the recent proclamation. "I think your father is right. Japan is being crushed."

"How can Japan be getting weaker when there are so many more Japanese police here?"

"They're just trying to make us think they're still in charge."

"But they *are* still in charge." Lily could feel herself growing irritated with her best friend.

Susie would not let up. "The reports are saying that's just not true. Japan is losing the war in the Pacific."

"You're wrong, Susie. Japan hasn't given up." This was turning into an argument that Lily didn't want to have. She wanted Susie to agree with her and understand how endless this war felt. Why was Susie being so stubborn when they both knew that at the end of most streets leading out of the ghetto, there were armed Japanese units posted behind barbed wire barriers? Pop always said that these barbed wire walls were hardly necessary. He said if a face like his was seen on the other side of Shanghai, everyone would know he was a Jew – it would be next to impossible to hide. Up until her recent encounter with the Japanese police, Lily had rarely thought about the guards, or about the blockades that kept the Jews in. Now she felt as if she had to look over her shoulder to make sure there wasn't a soldier approaching from behind. From now on, she would avoid any streets that led past the barricades.

The loud drone of airplanes filled the air. They were a new occurrence over Hongkew. "You see?" Lily shouted over the roar of the plane engines. "How can things be good when there are bombers flying over our heads?"

Susie pulled Lily to a stop and grabbed her by the shoulders. Her face was only inches from Lily's. "They're American bombers," Susie shouted. "It's another good sign. The more of those planes we see, the better!"

Lily pulled free and pushed past Susie. She'd had enough of this. She walked quickly ahead, glancing up at the sky and at the squadron of planes flying past. She wanted to believe that her father and Susie were right, and that American planes above Shanghai were a good sign. She wanted thousands more American bombers to fill the skies above Hongkew and bring an end to the war. But it still felt unlikely.

What did Susie think was going to happen? Were they going to wake up one morning and find the Japanese soldiers gone? *Impossible!*

Lily began to pick up her pace, swerving to avoid a mountain of muck and garbage that lay steaming on the sidewalk. She could feel Susie on her heels, but she wasn't ready to talk just yet. Then, just as she was passing an empty yard next to the school, Susie gasped behind her and reached out to grab Lily's arm. Lily was about to shake free when the look on Susie's face stopped her. Her eyes followed Susie's pointing finger. There, in the middle of some weeds and scattered bits of garbage, was the body of a child. It was a Chinese girl, probably just a few years younger than Lily. The girl's arms and legs were twisted at awkward angles. The child's head was completely severed from her body and lay to one side, as if it had been tossed there like a forgotten ball. Flies were already beginning to gather on the remains.

Lily and Susie stood silently and stared at the lifeless little girl. Lily wasn't scared or even horrified. People died in the ghetto on a daily basis, often forgotten and discarded in alleys and empty fields, just like this child. Soon, coolies pulling carts would come to remove this body, as they came every day for other bodies that had been abandoned in the ghetto. She felt sad for this small child who had been left here to rot. She wondered how the girl had died and if she had been in pain. She wondered if this child had friends that she used to play with, a mother who had worked every day, and a father who had tried to take care of his family and had promised that everyone would be safe.

Lily and Susie could disagree all they wanted about the future of the war. The truth was, they were still in the middle of it. Hongkew was real. Disease and death were real. The Japanese police were real. Their imprisonment was real!

Later that evening, Lily stared out the window at the road below her apartment. There was a funeral procession passing by. Men and women were dressed in white, as was the Chinese custom whenever there was a funeral. They carried pictures of the person who had died. Several men held small stringed instruments that they strummed to accompany the women who cried out with long, loud wails. Lily wondered if they were crying for the little girl she had seen earlier that day. She could feel that painful knot in her stomach – the one she always felt when events around her were upsetting. She hated this feeling. She longed to trust her father and Susie when they said that they were all going to be safe. But it was hard to believe in the end of a war when death was all around her.

Chapter 21

January, 1945

Over the next few months, the news that arrived from Europe continued to take Lily and the other Jewish refugees on an emotional roller coaster. In late August 1944, U.S. and British forces entered the city of Paris and liberated it from Nazi control. In October, the Nazi army, under pressure from the Allies, began to withdraw from Athens, Greece. This was quickly followed by a massive surrender of Nazi troops at the city of Aachen in the western part of Germany. With each new Allied victory, Lily's family would gather around their forbidden radio to celebrate the news and toast the possibility of an end to the war. Mom and Pop's faces shone with anticipation that the next broadcast would bring news of still more Nazi defeats. That excitement was cut short in January, 1945.

It was another winter day in Hongkew. Lily was dazed by the realization that they were closing in on two long years of imprisonment. Pop had gone out to get a copy of the *Shanghai Jewish Chronicle*, one of the many newspapers published in the ghetto. Lily was helping her mother clean the apartment. She pulled the woollen scarf tighter around her neck and bent over the straw broom. No matter how hard Mom tried to disinfect their flat, the dirt and grime somehow found its way back inside. Even in the winter, mold grew on the walls, sprouting like a vegetable garden underneath the window and down to the floor. The Chinese amahs would come to scrub the slimy, green moss away. But like clockwork, Lily knew it would be back the next day.

Pop came in just as Lily was sweeping the last of the fine grit from the floor. He walked past her, barely noticing that she was there, and sat heavily at the table.

"Fritz?" Mom sounded alarmed and Lily raised her eyes to her father's face. He was white and sweating. "Tell me what it is," demanded Mom.

At first, Pop couldn't speak. Lily couldn't begin to imagine what bad news he had brought home. Finally, he laid the newspaper on the table and slumped over it. Mom and Lily moved to peer over his shoulder. There, on the front page, was a picture so gruesome that at first, Lily could barely comprehend what she was seeing; ghostlike men, women, and children with sticks for arms and legs. Their faces were so thin and shrunken that they almost didn't look human. These skeletal figures were huddled together under blankets and stared at the camera through blank, lifeless eyes. The headline above the photo proclaimed: AUSCHWITZ LIBERATED.

"It's another concentration camp." Pop whispered so softly that Lily had to bend closer to the horrifying picture just to hear him. Now, the wasted figures were practically in her face. "No, not just another one," continued Pop. "They say it's the biggest one the Nazis built. They say that more than a million Jews may have been murdered there."

Lily stared at the picture. It was terrifying enough to *hear* the news on the radio of thousands and even millions of Jews being killed in these death camps. But to *see* the faces of those who had been held captive, filled Lily with such dread that her knees went weak, and her head began to spin. She too had to sit down.

The photographs that followed in the next few weeks were even more gruesome and more unbelievable. There were pictures of gas chambers and ovens and mass graves with detailed explanations of how and where Jews had been killed across Europe.

"What kind of disturbed mind could have thought of such ways to murder innocent people?" Pop would say, shaking his head as each new photograph appeared. Lily turned away. She couldn't look anymore. After each newspaper article appeared, she would leave the apartment to go and talk to Susie. The two girls had patched up their earlier disagreement. These days, they sought each other out more often. It was difficult to talk to Mom and Pop. They were consumed with the war news and barely noticed Lily as she went about her day. But even Susie, with her hopeful outlook for the end of the war, could offer little comfort or explanation in the face of the news and the magnitude of the losses. Often the two girls just sat on the stoop in front of Susie's apartment, saying nothing, and watching the citizens of Hongkew trudge by.

Lily was returning from one of those afternoons at Susie's place. It was late, and the sky was growing dark. Lily knew that Pop hated it when she got home after dusk. He worried about her being on the streets at that time; these days, there were too many desperate people in the ghetto looking for an easy victim to mug and rob, not to mention the ever-present Japanese police.

Lily picked up her pace, winding her way through the dimly lit streets toward the SACRA. She was close to home now; just a few more turns and she would be there. She wondered if Mom would have a decent meal waiting for her at home. These days, Mom often made a disgusting concoction of spinach mixed with one egg and a bit of milk. "Eat it up," she would say. "It's healthy and will put meat on your bones." Lily would stare at the plate. The smell was horrible and the taste was even worse. She would have to hold her nose to place a forkful in her mouth, and she still gagged with each bite.

Lily wrapped her beautiful red cape closer around her body. Mom had bought it for her as a special treat, and Lily loved it, though it didn't provide quite enough protection from the cold February wind. Up ahead she could see her apartment and wondered if Pop would be leaning out the window, straining to see if she was coming. She knew he wouldn't be angry with her, especially if she explained that she had been with Susie. Still, she hated to make him worry.

Finally, she was home. She pushed open the doors of the building and began to race up the long staircase. Perhaps her mind was still on the conversation she would have with her father to explain why she was late. Maybe she was thinking about the dinner that Mom would have on the table and how she could avoid the spinach mixture. But it was probably the long cape that simply got in the way of Lily's quick sprint up the stairs. With just a few steps left to go, her foot became twisted in the folds of fabric. She suddenly pitched forward without having enough time to catch herself. The next thing she knew, her head had bounced off the top step, and she was tumbling head over heels down the stairs. She came to an abrupt stop in a heap at the bottom.

Lily lay there, stunned. The red cape was rolled around her body like a tight blanket. It took a second to free her arm and when she finally did, she reached up to touch her head. When she pulled her hand away, it was covered in blood.

Lily didn't remember screaming out. But she must have because within seconds, Pop was in the stairwell by her side. He scooped her into his arms and rushed up the stairs, past the curious residents who had come into the hallway to see what had happened. Inside their apartment, Pop laid Lily gently on his bed. By now she was wailing, partly from the scare of seeing so much blood and partly from the pain that was growing more intense by the second. It didn't help that Pop, usually so calm, looked terrified.

Mom appeared, knelt by the side of the bed, and laid a towel across Lily's head. Lily continued to scream, and the bleeding would not stop. Each towel came away soaked and red. Finally, Mom and Pop looked at each other. "We need to get a doctor," said Pop, still stroking Lily's arm. "I'll go find Dr. Didner."

Dr. Sam Didner was one of several doctors treating every disease possible in Hongkew. He treated eye infections and ringworm and dysentery, and even more serious ailments like meningitis, mostly without the benefit of medications, which had long since been used up in the ghetto. He was a well-known sight, riding his bicycle through the alleys, on his way to or from a patient visit. By the time Pop returned with the doctor, Lily had calmed down a bit. Her head still throbbed and there was still a steady stream of blood flowing from the wound. But her screams had been replaced with small, rapid hiccups. The sight of the doctor in their apartment brought on a fresh gush of tears.

"Now, now, Lily," said Dr. Didner, as he approached the bed and bent over her. His bicycle stood in a corner. He was known to drag the bike wherever he went, up and down apartment staircases, always worried that it might be stolen if he left it on the street during a house call. "I'll be very careful and you tell me if I hurt you."

The doctor lifted the soggy towel to examine Lily's forehead. His fingers were gentle as he probed the injured area and peered at the gash. He stood a few minutes later and looked into her eyes. "That's quite a cut you have," he said. "I'm afraid I'm going to have to stitch it."

There was something about the doctor's tender touch and easy manner that calmed Lily even in the face of this verdict. "Will it hurt?" she asked.

Dr. Didner adjusted the black bow tie that he always wore and cleared his throat. "I won't lie to you. It's going to be painful and you're going to have to be very brave."

Lily gulped back a few more tears. Pop was by her side in an instant. "Is there nothing you can give her?" he asked. Lily could feel his hand trembling as he grabbed hers.

The doctor shook his head and motioned to Lily's parents to follow him over to the other side of the room. It was easy for Lily to hear what the grown-ups were whispering in the small space. "There is no pain medication available for cases like this," Dr. Didner began. "The little that we have is in the General Hospital, reserved for patients with far more serious injuries. I'm not worried about the stitching;

we'll get Lily through that. I'm more concerned about the possibility of infection afterwards. I have no medication for that, either."

Lily closed her eyes. She had heard stories about other refugees who had injured themselves. Without drugs to treat the wounds, some had even died from the infection that set it. *No!* thought Lily. *I can't think of that. It's too scary.* When she opened her eyes, Dr. Didner was standing over her again.

"I'm going to wipe the area clean, Lily. You hold onto your parents while I sew this up."

Minutes later, it was all over. Lily had clutched Mom's arm so tightly during the stitching that she had left a red mark there. But she had not cried out even once. Dr. Didner covered the stitches with a white cloth bandage and gave Mom some instructions on how to dress and clean the area.

"We can try some Chinese herbs to dull the pain and treat the cut. I'll bring some by tomorrow," he said, as he packed up his kit and picked up his bicycle. "Watch it carefully. If there is any redness or swelling, let me know right away."

"How can we pay you, Doctor?" Pop began. "We don't have much…."

Dr. Didner brushed the question aside. "I don't need payment. I'm glad I could help. Good-bye, Lily. You are a very courageous girl."

Lily managed a weak smile. She was exhausted after her ordeal. All she wanted was to close her eyes and try to forget about everything.

That night she slept with Mom, while Pop took the cot. She knew that both her parents would spend most of the night taking turns watching over her – just as they always did.

Chapter 22

Dr. Didner came by several more times over the next few weeks to check on Lily, and happily, her injury healed well. There was no infection and before long, she was her usual self, going to school, spending time with Susie, and helping her parents in the apartment. They breathed a sigh of relief as Lily's wound began to heal. Eventually, all that was left was a pink scar.

"It's a good sign," Pop said. "Mom bounced back from her fight with the Japanese police, and you are completely fine after your fall. Now, with luck, the war will soon be over, too."

Indeed, on a daily basis, the radio and newspapers were bringing more and more encouraging reports about the end of the war. On May 1, 1945, Nazi forces laid down their arms to the Allies in Italy. On May 2, the Nazis surrendered in Berlin. This was followed by defeats in Denmark and the Netherlands. Then came the news that Adolf Hitler, realizing his troops were on the verge of being overthrown, had taken his own life in a bunker in Germany. Pop read this newspaper article out loud to Lily and Mom and remarked bitterly, "Suicide was too good for him. He should have been brought to trial."

"At least he's gone," replied Mom. And Lily couldn't have agreed more.

May 7 brought the news that everyone had prayed for. All remaining Nazi forces across Europe had yielded to the Allied armies and had signed final surrender documents at Reims in France. The radio reports on May 8 declared that day to be V-E Day – Victory in Europe day!

There were celebrations across the ghetto as Jewish families took to the streets shouting and cheering at the news. Even the usually visible Japanese police faded into the background that day, allowing the residents of Hongkew to rejoice in the end of the war. Pop's eyes shone as he talked about what this would mean for them and all the Jewish refugees.

"It's what we've prayed for, Lily!" he said. "After six long years of war in Europe, it's finally over."

"Perhaps now we can find out what has become of our friends. I can only hope that some have survived," added Mom. "Maybe we can even go back to Vienna." Her voice was breathless with hope.

"First things first," said Pop. "The war in the Pacific has to come to an end. But Japan will be the next to fall," he said. "Now that the

Nazis have been defeated, the Japanese armies will surrender. It will happen soon."

"And then we'll be free, Pop?" asked Lily.

"Yes," he replied. "We will be free."

It was the first time her father had actually said those words aloud. And for a moment, Lily did not know how to respond. What would it mean to be free, she wondered – to walk out of Hongkew without having to show a pass card, without having to fear the Japanese police. What would it mean to be able to shop in stores wherever she wanted, to have warm clothing in winter, and to have enough food so that her stomach didn't cry out in hunger? What would it mean to leave China and go somewhere else? She couldn't even guess where that might be. Back to Vienna? Across the ocean to America? The truth is, she and the other refugee families had never really "chosen" Shanghai as a destination at the start of the war. And Shanghai had never really been prepared to accept as many Jews as it did. As thankful as they all were to have escaped from Europe and to have found a place willing to take them in, the opportunity to choose where they would live had been taken from Lily's family years earlier. Now, they might have a choice about their future for the first time. It was something Lily hardly dared dream about.

But freedom didn't come as quickly as Lily and her parents had hoped. Over the next few months, everyone in the ghetto held their breath, waiting for the Japanese soldiers to disappear from the streets of Hongkew. That didn't happen. The barricades remained in place, the police continued to patrol, and the newspapers reported that the Japanese army refused to surrender. When Lily questioned her father about this, he shook his head and replied, "Japan is saying it will fight to the bitter end."

The end of what? Aren't things bitter enough? The fighting had already gone on for far too long as far as Lily was concerned. Too many people had been killed. Too much of her life had been spent living in this imprisonment. Yet the freedom to go wherever and whenever she wanted seemed as distant as ever. War made no sense to her.

By early July, frightening new rumors sent the refugees of Hongkew into a fresh round of panic. Willi arrived to deliver the news early one morning just as Lily was halfway out the door and heading off to school. His dog, Meckie, was with him as always, panting and begging for a scrap of food. Lily stopped to scratch behind Meckie's ear.

"I'm on patrol this morning, but I needed to come here first to talk to you," Willi said as he pointed to the white cloth band that encircled his arm. Recently, Willi had been ordered to become part of a new group in Hongkew called the *Pao Chia*, a collection of Jewish men who had been commanded by the Japanese military to become a patrolling unit on their behalf. The Pao Chia were meant to guard the streets of Hongkew, check to make sure that the refugees had their identification papers, and report any violation of rules to their Japanese commanders, including General Ghoya. In the beginning,

Many men, like Lily's Uncle Willi, were forced to become members of the Pao Chia. They wore this band on their arm.

上海公共租界
外人保甲自警團
第　　　保
FOREIGN PAO CHIA
VIGILANCE CORPS
PAO

520

Willi said that he would never agree to join. "I refuse to become one of their puppets," he had stated passionately. "I won't do the dirty work for them." But the family had urged him to sign up, knowing that the punishment for refusing would be severe. Willi finally agreed, though he swore that he would never inform on his fellow Jews. The white band had become a familiar sight on the arms of many young men in the ghetto.

"I don't know if we should believe any of this," Willi began, "but I thought you should know. The Japanese army has produced a list of the Jewish refugees in Hongkew. They say we're going to be rounded up, put on boats, and taken to a deserted island across the river."

Lily was still busy playing with Meckie, but she stopped and looked up when she heard her uncle deliver this message. "What's on the island?"

Willi glanced back at Lily's parents before replying. "They've built prison camps over there. At least that's what I've heard."

Mom gasped. "That's exactly what the Nazis did to the Jews in Europe."

"Willi, are we going to go into prisons?" Lily rose from the floor. Memories of shocking newspaper photos flashed before her eyes.

"Nothing is for sure," Willi said.

"But you wouldn't have come to tell us about it if you hadn't thought it was true," Lily persisted.

"First the ghetto, then the prisons, then who knows what...."

Mom whispered this and then looked up to stare into Lily's wide eyes.

"You know how people get when there's a rumor," Willi continued, softer this time. "Some of this stuff is just meant to scare us."

If the Japanese army wants to scare me, then they are doing a good job of it, Lily thought.

Willi whistled to Meckie to follow him out the door. "I'll see if I can find out anything more from the other Pao Chia. For now, just try and avoid any Japanese patrols on the streets."

Lily didn't need to be reminded of that.

"Perhaps we should walk you to school," Pop said, as Lily paused at the door once more.

She shook her head. "I'm not a baby, Pop. I'll be fine." She didn't want her parents to see that this new information had shaken her. They had enough to worry about. She would have to be scared and brave at the same time. But when she left the apartment, Lily could see that news of the prison camps had already reached the streets of Hongkew. Groups of men and women huddled on street corners, their heads bent together in whispered conversations. When Lily walked past a newspaper stand, she read the bold front-page headline: JEWS TO BE TRANSPORTED TO PRISON CAMPS. Her breath quickened along with her heartbeat.

Later that evening, the whole family gathered at the apartment to talk about this new threat. Lily disappeared into a darkened corner. The less visible she was, the more her family felt free to talk. Lily wanted to make sure she heard every word that they were saying. No more half-truths or whispered warnings.

"It's on the island of Woosung," Willi said. "There's already a prison camp there for Americans who were captured after the bombing of Pearl Harbor. Now it's all set for the rest of us."

"Did you see the empty boats in the harbor?" Aunt Stella asked. "They're waiting for the Japanese commanders to give the order to load us on."

Willi nodded forcefully. "The lists that they've posted are incomplete," he said. "The Japanese police want us to add our names."

"I won't sign a paper that might lead to our arrest – or worse," Pop replied.

"There's not one Jewish person in Hongkew who will submit to this order," Willi continued, thumping on the table with a clenched fist. "We'll fight back before we're arrested." The others murmured their agreement.

"Fight?" Aunt Nini spoke up. "Fight with what? Sticks against guns will do little good." This comment brought the conversation to a dead halt.

Even in the midst of her family members, Lily felt alone and scared. *This can't be happening*, she thought. Just weeks earlier there had been celebrations in Hongkew after the victory of the Allies over the Nazis. *Hitler is dead! Pop said we would be free, soon.* Lily had let herself believe that things were getting better, not worse.

"If they come for us, we'll escape." Aunt Stella had risen from her seat at the table, and was pacing back and forth in the tiny flat. "We'll go back to Frenchtown and hide out there."

"Where do you think we can hide?" Willi asked. "If we're caught without papers on the other side, they'll do much worse than arrest us." At this, he slid his finger slowly across his throat. Aunt Stella gasped and sank back onto her chair.

"Perhaps the nuns could hide us at the convent," Mom suggested. "I could ask."

Pop shook his head. "I don't think we want to put them in such a dangerous position."

Once again, the room went silent. A fly hovered around the light bulb that hung from the ceiling. The only sound that could be heard was the faint buzzing of its wings and a small pop each time it hit the bulb and recoiled. Finally, Pop sat up tall in his chair and looked around the room, taking in every member of the family, including Lily. When he spoke, his voice was strong and clear. "Each day that passes is a day that brings us closer to the end of our imprisonment. All we can hope for now is for time to be on our side." He leaned forward and dropped his voice to a whisper. "Whatever happens, and whatever we do, we stay together."

At this, they all nodded in solemn agreement.

Chapter 23

July 17, 1945

The newspapers articles that appeared in the following weeks brought even more uncertainty to the Jews of Hongkew. Some proclaimed that Woosung Island was ready and waiting for its Jewish prisoners. Others talked about the arrest of Japanese commanders and the liberation of the ghetto. After a while, Lily began to avoid the radio and the newspapers. They only frustrated her with their announcements of victories by the Allies, followed by grim reports about casualties, along with rumors of new threats.

The end of the war is what Lily was thinking about on July 17, as she sat with her mother having lunch. The air in the apartment was heavy and hot. Mom was fanning herself absentmindedly with a folded newspaper. Still, sweat glistened on her forehead and ran down her face and neck in little rivers, soaking the front of her dress. Lily waved away the flies that buzzed around her head and turned back to her lunch. The beans were only marginally better than the spinach mixture Mom usually made, but Lily didn't complain. Still, she longed for real food.

The sound of an airplane engine rumbled in the distance. Lily wondered if it was one of many American planes making its journey over Shanghai. Lately there had been more and more of these planes and Lily, along with everyone else, wondered what that meant. "It has to be good news," Pop continued to say. But Lily would only shrug her shoulders and avoid that conversation.

The plane seemed to be coming closer. And now Lily thought that it had been joined by a second and possibly even a third. The roar of the engine was swelling. A rumbling tremor filled the apartment, starting in Lily's feet and working its way up her legs and into her stomach and arms. Even her plate was beginning to rattle on the table, as if she was shaking it. This had never happened before. Lily sat up in her chair as the thunder of the engines grew more threatening. Now it felt as if the planes were practically on top of their flat. Mom rose suddenly and rushed to the window just as Lily heard a low whistling sound from somewhere above. Mom paused and turned to face her daughter. The whistling grew sharper and more piercing. Mom and Lily locked eyes. The last thing Lily remembered was her mother screaming, "Lily, get down!"

In that second, a thunderous crash sent Lily and her mother tumbling onto the floor. Lily screamed and clutched at the leg of her chair, as chunks of plaster began to fall on top of her from the ceiling. The window pane shook violently and then shattered, flinging shards of glass across the room. Mom reached out, and, with one hand, she pulled her daughter under the table. The other hand reached for the mattress from the bed, which she hauled on top of them. Lily and her mother huddled there as the floor shook and heaved beneath their bodies.

"Mom, what is it?" Lily cried. She had curled her body into a ball and was shielding her head with her arms. The table bounced up and down above her.

"A bomb – from the airplane." The sound of engines still thundered, and Mom had to yell into Lily's ear to be heard. Plaster continued to fall from the walls and ceiling. "We need to get out of here," shouted Mom. "There may be more."

With that, Mom shoved the mattress aside and struggled to her feet. She grabbed Lily, and the two of them stumbled to the door and out into the hallway. Other people were already there, pushing and shoving to get down the stairs. Lily held tightly to her mother and followed her onto the street. It was bedlam outside. People ran in all directions, shrieking, covering their heads, and pointing above them. The sky was a hazy gray, but dozens of planes were emerging from behind the thick clouds and circling overhead, coming ever so much closer by the second. And when Lily looked up, she was horrified to see the flag of the United States painted prominently on the front of the bombers. *What are the Americans doing? They are supposed to be coming to rescue us, not kill us!* But Lily could see the cargo doors of these planes opening and black bombs cascading toward the ground. The sound of roaring engines mixed with screams rang in Lily's ears, and thick smoke filled her lungs. A second explosion sounded close by. Bricks and garbage and fragments of buildings rained down from above, sending the already terrified crowd into a new frenzy.

"We need to find a safe place!" Mom was still pulling Lily, trying desperately to get through the roadblock of people.

An old woman pushed past Lily and her mother. "Run to the kitchen!" she shrieked.

Lily glanced over at the kitchen building next to the SACRA. She could see that dozens of people were pushing through the doorway, trying to get inside the small wooden structure.

"Mom! In there?"

Mom shook her head. "It will never hold," she shouted.

Lily looked around, searching for a place that could protect them. Her eyes finally rested on the small concrete building on the other side of the courtyard. Harry had pointed it out to her on the first day she had moved into the SACRA. "It's a bomb shelter," he had said. At the time she had barely shown interest.

Lily tugged on her mother's arm and pointed. Mom's eyes followed

Lily's hand. She nodded, and the two of them sprinted across the yard and toward the building. It was almost completely filled with people when they pushed through the door and found a place to crouch against the wall. They huddled there, arms around each other, saying nothing. An old man next to Lily wheezed loudly, trying to catch his breath. A young boy cried out. Fear, like an icy wind, swept across the room and held everyone in its tight grip.

Where's Pop? Lily wondered. *Is he still in the shop? Did he find a safe place to hide? And what about Willi, and my other aunts and uncles?* Lily didn't want to consider the possibility that her father or any of her relatives had been caught in the bombing, but she couldn't stop from thinking the worst. She worried about Susie and Harry and all the other students in her school. It would be impossible for all of them to find solid shelter within the confines of the ghetto.

Another explosion rocked the bomb shelter from side to side. Several people screamed and clutched at the walls of the building and at each other. Dust floated down from the ceiling. Lily closed her eyes and buried her head in her mother's shoulder. She reached up to cover her ears with her hands, trying to block out the sound of blasts and cries. Mom held Lily tightly and stroked her head, whispering, "Sh, it will be fine. We'll be fine." But Mom's voice shook and trembled almost as much as the building in which they were huddled.

Lily didn't know how long they sat in the shelter as bombs exploded all around them. At one point she realized it must be night time; the slivers of light that had filtered underneath the shelter door disappeared, and darkness shrouded everyone inside. It was only as new light was beginning to trickle in that the sounds of explosions from outside began to fade and then finally disappeared. For a while, no one moved. No one dared to believe that the danger had passed and they were safe. Finally, a young man stumbled to the door and pushed it open. He turned to face the others. "I think the coast is clear," he said. Lily and Mom rose, still holding each other, and followed the other refugees out onto the streets.

Chapter 24

The sight that greeted Lily when they emerged from the bomb shelter was enough to make her want to turn and run back inside. In the early hours of the new morning, the Hongkew ghetto looked as if it had been hit by an earthquake. Bricks, wood, and glass lay in piles of rubble where buildings had once stood. Other smaller houses had fallen against one another like tiles in a game of dominos. Rickshaws and carts were overturned and abandoned on the road. Small fires burned everywhere and smoke billowed into clouds, filling the air above Lily's head. People walked by, looking stunned and confused, shaking their heads and muttering incomprehensible words under their breath. Some were bleeding, but they hardly seemed to notice their wounds. Others lay, barely moving, on what was left of the sidewalks. The sounds of crying and moaning came from all around.

Lily held her mother's hand and stepped carefully over jagged pieces of glass, smoldering wood, and other debris. She glanced over at their apartment building and gasped out loud. It was still standing, but just barely. The windows were gone, blown out by the force of the explosions. Staircases dangled in mid-air. Where several walls had once been, there were now just the empty shells of small rooms, staring back at her. It was as if someone had sliced away a portion of the SACRA, opening it like a book to expose the inside. The whole building tilted dangerously to one side.

Lily stumbled over a small crater in the courtyard and caught herself. And then she heard her mother cry out and turned to follow her gaze. The small kitchen that had stood next to their apartment building – the first place Lily had wanted to take shelter – was gone. All that was left was a smoking heap of wooden planks.

"Mom!" she cried. "What about all the people who went in there?"

Mom's hand flew up to her throat. "They must be trapped…or gone," she whispered.

And then, as she and her mother stood surveying the damage that had been done to their neighborhood, they heard a familiar voice frantically calling out to them. It was Pop!

"Lily! Erna! Oh, thank goodness you are all right. I've been frantic with worry." Pop reached his wife and daughter and grabbed them, pulling them close and gripping them so tightly that Lily had to pull away to catch her breath. Pop was shaking almost as much as she was. She gazed up at her father. She had never been so happy to see him.

"This part of the ghetto was hit the worst," he said. "I didn't know what to do when I wasn't able to reach you yesterday." He choked out these last words.

"Pop, what about Uncle Willi?" Lily was almost afraid to ask about her family members.

"Willi's fine," Pop replied. "He was with me at the shop. Nothing was hit around us even though we could see the explosions in the distance." Pop glanced at his wife. "He's gone to look for the others. I pray they're safe as well."

Mom sobbed, unable to speak. "How could this have happened?" she finally blurted out.

Pop pointed to the brick wall that had once stood behind their apartment building. It too had been reduced to rubble. "They say that the American bombers were aiming at the radio tower behind our apartment building. The Japanese army may have been hiding arms and munitions back there, thinking that the Americans would never bomb an area with so many Chinese and Jewish refugees. But war is war," he added bitterly. "Who knows how many innocent people have been injured or killed in this?"

Lily glanced once more at the toppled kitchen, wondering if anyone could have survived under the crush of the building. Then she heard another voice calling their names. She turned to see her Uncle

Willi striding up the road toward them. Meckie was running by his side.

"They're all fine," he said, even before Mom could ask the question. "Nini and Poldi. Walter and Stella. Their apartment buildings were damaged from the shock of the explosions, but they didn't take a direct hit. Not like this." He gazed up at what was left of the SACRA and then turned back to Lily and her parents. "We are all so lucky," he added, giving Lily a quick squeeze around the shoulders. It was probably the closest he had ever come to hugging her.

"I can't stay," Willi said. "I need to go and help with the rescue. All the Pao Chia men are organizing to help." He pointed at the white cloth band on his arm. "I don't mind giving a hand this time." He stared at the collapsed kitchen and shook his head. "There's a lot to clean up, and I'll do anything to help rescue anybody who's still alive."

Lily tugged on her uncle's arm, and he bent to stare into her eyes. "Please, be careful."

Willi smiled. "Believe me, I won't do anything stupid."

"It's a miracle that none of us were hurt, and I want it to stay that way," added Pop. And with that, Willi turned and headed off down the street. Meckie was by his heels.

"Now then," Pop said, once Willi had turned a corner and disappeared, "let's figure out what we're going to do."

There was no way they could return to their apartment. The building was so unstable it appeared as if the slightest wind would topple it to the ground. But they did need to find some shelter. For the next few hours, Lily and her parents stumbled around the courtyard of the SACRA, picking up discarded blankets and sheets to fashion a makeshift campsite for the night. They were not alone. Other Jewish and Chinese families scavenged for provisions right next to them. And for the first time that Lily could remember, the Jewish and Chinese residents of Hongkew helped one another find supplies to get through the next few days. Both groups had endured this disaster, and now they were working side by side, supporting each other in dealing with it. A cart appeared out of nowhere, and an old Chinese gentleman began to pass out steaming bowls of rice. Lily gratefully accepted one and gulped the food down, suddenly realizing how ravenous she was. She had not eaten in more than a day. Someone else carted in clean, boiled water so that people could line up to drink and wash the dirt and soot from their faces and hands.

Lily recognized Dr. Didner running through the crowd, passing out bandages, and treating cuts and gashes. Occasionally, he would stoop over a figure that had not moved in some time. Then Lily watched him call out to some fit-looking men for help. As a lifeless body was lifted, everyone would stop what they were doing, bow their heads, and wait for the procession to pass. Instinctively, Lily reached up to touch the raised scar on her forehead. That injury seemed so insignificant now.

By the time the day had ended, Lily and her parents had collected enough necessities to make it through that night. They staked out a spot in the field next to the SACRA. Even though the night time air was still hot, several people had lit small campfires that illuminated the courtyard. Lily stretched out on a blanket and laid her head in her mother's lap. She looked up at the sky, which was alight with millions of stars. They sparkled down on the Hongkew ghetto, casting an eerie glow upon the devastation. Here and there, a shooting star erupted in a bright spark and then faded to nothing. The stars were comforting. They reminded Lily that the world was still turning, and some things were still normal. She still didn't know what had happened to Susie or Harry or her other school friends. First thing tomorrow, she would try to find them. She didn't know how or where they would be living from now on, but she was certain that her parents would take care of her, just as they always did. Despite everything that had happened in the last two days, Lily felt strangely calm. She was still alive. Her parents were still alive, and so were her aunts and uncles. They were still together, just like Pop said they would always be.

Chapter 25

Susie came looking for Lily first. Almost as soon as she opened her eyes the next morning, Lily could see her friend walking up the street toward what was left of the SACRA. Even from a distance, Lily could see the alarm written across her friend's face. Lily leapt from the ground and ran to meet her. The two young girls hugged each other warmly.

"I wanted to come yesterday, but my parents wouldn't let me out of our apartment," Susie said.

"I was worried about you, too."

"Our place wasn't hit, even though there was a lot of noise and shaking. But this…" Susie gestured to the wreckage of Lily's apartment building. "How did you ever get through it?"

Lily described the events of the previous day including the last minute decision to run for the bomb shelter instead of the kitchen.

Susie listened, her eyes wide and solemn. "They're saying that hundreds of people were hurt or killed yesterday."

"And that could have been us, too," replied Lily. "It's a miracle that my whole family is still here." She had been saying that a lot lately, realizing that the line between life and death was so fine – an instantaneous choice to go this way or that. Yesterday, they had chosen well. Would they always be that lucky?

"We're going to be able to stay in our apartment. But what about you?" Susie's voice broke into Lily's thoughts.

Lily shrugged. "I have no idea. But my father is already out looking."

Pop had arisen before dawn and set out on a mission to find a new place for his family to live. Just before noon, Lily saw him striding up the street toward their spot in the courtyard with that calm, confident look once more restored to his face.

"Here's the news," he said. "I've found us a place to stay. We're going to move into the Kadoorie School. They are setting it up for Jewish families who lost their homes in the bombing." Pop paused as Lily looked at him expectantly. "But that means no more school for you, Lily – at least not for the time being."

Lily paused, and then a slow smile began to tug at the corners of her mouth. *No more school!* That meant no more Mr. Meyer and his laps around the courtyard, no more geometry, no more threat of the ruler across her knuckles. This was perhaps the best news she had received in a long time! She jumped up and hugged her father tightly around the neck.

"Don't worry, Pop," she said. "I promise I'll read every day. I'll even come and help you in the shoe store if you'd like."

Her father patted her back. "I'm not sure there will be much work at the shop. We'll just have to see what happens now."

It took no time for Lily and her parents to move into the Kadoorie School. After all, there was no furniture to move; no mattresses, chairs, or pots and pans. Some of their clothing had been salvaged from the sagging apartment building, but that was it. Miraculously, Mom's sewing machine had not been lost in the bombing of the SACRA. Lily's father was able to retrieve it and bring it along.

Other Jewish families and groups came to their aid, providing blankets, plates, and clothing to those who had nothing. The JDC, the same organization that had being providing a soup kitchen inside the ghetto for Jewish refugees, ramped up its efforts to obtain aid from the International Red Cross. Inside the school, cots were placed in all of the classrooms and the Jewish families were assigned beds where they would be sleeping, many to a room. Lily and her family were luckier than most. Instead of sharing a space with others, they were directed to a small more private hallway where two beds had been placed side by side across from a row of windows. The windows, however, would not provide any light. They were covered in blackout material. The

Japanese army had ordered this so that the ghetto would be less visible to any future bombers. A thin wooden screen that had been placed next to their cots was meant to separate this space from another family. Lily was delighted to discover that her friend Harry would be staying on the other side of the partition. She met up with Harry while she was standing on the street in a long food line.

"My parents and I were visiting with relatives on the other side of Hongkew when the bombs fell," Harry explained when Lily asked how he had managed to stay safe. "I thought about you," he added. "I heard that so many people had been killed. I didn't know if you'd made it or not."

The reports about casualties from the attack were rolling in, and they were devastating. Thirty-eight Jewish refugees had died in the bombing, most of them buried under buildings that had buckled on top of them, just like the kitchen building next to Lily's apartment. But that didn't even come close to the number of Chinese citizens who had been killed. Dr. Didner rushed past that morning to report that the number of Chinese deaths was already more than two hundred. And that was just an early count.

"Then there are the wounded," he said. "More than five hundred – both Jewish and Chinese. I can't possibly treat everyone." Dr. Didner's clothes were stained with blood and dirt. It looked as if he hadn't slept in days. But before Lily could say anything, he hurried off, muttering about how he needed to visit the sick.

Lily and Harry continued to wind their way along the street to the front of the line where hot soup was being spooned into small tin pots and passed to the refugees. Once again, some of the food had been brought in by Chinese citizens who were giving up the little they had to help their Jewish neighbors. Even though the Chinese had suffered so much in the bombing, they too, were hoping for an American victory in the war against their Japanese oppressors.

"My father told me that more than two hundred and fifty bombs were dropped on Shanghai," Lily said. Even in the Kadoorie School, someone had managed to produce a shortwave radio. Most of the refugees could be found listening to the reports that trickled in about the bombing.

"And there could be more," Harry added. "It's a fight to the finish now. The Americans won't give up, and the Japanese won't give in."

That day, there were still Japanese police troops patrolling along the streets where Lily and Harry were lined up for food. But there was something different in how they were behaving. They continued to hold their guns at the ready, but the expressions on their faces were more uncertain, as if they sensed that this might be a turning point for the war and their future. Gone were their nasty sneers and threatening gestures.

It was still incredible to Lily that it was the Americans who had dropped these bombs on the ghetto and caused all the injuries and deaths. They were the very people who were supposed to be saving them! But Pop had said that's what happened in war. There were always innocent people caught in the middle of any battle. Lily shuddered. She didn't know if the ghetto could withstand another attack. She was terrified to relive what she had endured a few days earlier. The nightmare of the bombs dropping on top of the SACRA still played like a horror film through her mind whenever she closed her eyes.

Harry nudged her forward and Lily stepped up and held out her pot for some soup. She shook her head, not wanting to think about the bombing. There was nothing she could do about that or about the outcome of this war. For now, she would have to adjust to living in the Kadoorie School, lining up on the street for food, and praying for no more attacks.

When Lily returned to the school she could hear a hum coming from behind the partition where she and her parents were now living. When she entered their small space, she was startled to see her mother bent over the sewing machine. Its needle was fluttering up and down as Mom pushed some fabric across the metal plate.

"Are you going to work, Mom?" Lily asked.

Mom shook her head. "There is no work for me, right now," she replied. "The Japanese army has cancelled all of the permits that allow us out of Hongkew."

"Then what are you doing?" Lily pointed at the small squares of material that covered Mom's sewing machine.

"I'm making a new game for you," she replied, smiling. "You don't have school, and I don't have work. So we're all going to need some new activities."

Mom handed Lily a couple of two-inch patches of material that she had sewn together, leaving a small opening. "You fill this little pouch with some dirt from outside, and I'll finish stitching it up."

Before long, Lily and Mom had made a half dozen of these little sacks. Lily gathered Susie, Harry, and some of the other children at the school to try out the new game. The object was to throw all six pouches into the air at once, and to see how many you could catch with one hand. Before long, Harry had thought up another new game. He produced some empty cigarette boxes and dumped them onto the floor.

"Let's see who can throw a box the farthest," he said, picking one up and tossing it down the empty school hallway. It landed and slid across the floor. One by one, Lily and her friends lined up to see who could pitch their box farther than Harry's.

The next couple of days passed quickly as Lily and her friends invented game after game to occupy their time. Mom and Pop and several other parents were often there to watch from the sidelines. Like Mom, many other grown-ups were now unable to leave the ghetto and get to their jobs in Shanghai. Lily's father had pretty much closed up shop as well. Occasionally, he would go to the shoe store just to make sure there were no looters around trying to break in and steal the few supplies he had left. But no one was buying very much these days. Lily and her family were lucky to have the soup line and some shelter.

Even though the games inside the Kadoorie School were entertaining and passed the time, the dangers and bad news simply would not let up. Several days after they had moved into the school, Pop received word that Uncle Willi had been injured while helping to clear some debris from a building that had been bombed. Like Dr. Didner, Willi had not stopped helping in the rescue efforts. From morning until night, he had lifted wood and rocks, helped remove bodies from underneath collapsed structures, and carted food and provisions to refugees in need. But several days earlier, he had fallen while climbing over a pile of wreckage. Some jagged wires had cut deeply into Willi's leg.

"Dr. Didner stitched it, but I'm afraid it's become infected," Pop told Lily. "There's nothing the doctor can do to treat it."

They went over to see Willi that evening. He lay on his bed in Stella and Walter's apartment, eyes closed, breathing in shallow gulps. His skin was gray and sweat dotted his forehead. Meckie lay on the floor next to his master, whimpering softly for Willi to wake up. At first, Lily shrank away from her uncle. She had never seen him like this and it frightened her to see him so sick. Then, she took a deep breath and approached his bed, kneeling down in front of him.

"Please don't die, Uncle Willi," she whispered. "I'll even let you tell me some ghost stories. You can tease me all you want, and I won't care." Behind her, Lily could hear her aunts crying softly.

"I don't know if Willi's going to make it," Pop whispered. "You need to prepare yourself, Lily."

She pushed her father away, angrily. *This isn't supposed to happen. My family is going to stay together, just like you always promised.* "Don't listen to him, Willi. Just promise me you won't die," Lily repeated.

"He can't really hear you, darling." Mom had come to stand next to her daughter.

"You don't know that," Lily replied stubbornly.

Uncle Willi remained in a coma for days, hanging by a thread in that place between life and death. Lily and her parents visited as often as they could. And Lily continued to talk to her uncle, telling him stories about what new games her friends had invented at the Kadoorie School, what Harry or Susie or one of her other friends had said, what book she had found in the school library. Dr. Didner was there on one of Lily's visits. He looked worn down, as if he had witnessed too much death in the days since the bombing of Hongkew. Lily watched as he placed his hand on Willi's forehead, checking to see if the fever had broken. Then he stood up and shook his head.

"Can't you *please* help him?" Lily begged.

Dr. Didner sighed and turned away. "No medications. No supplies."

"But you helped me when I cut my forehead," Lily persisted. "There must be something you can do." Meckie whined softly from his watch on the floor.

"I wish there was more," Dr. Didner muttered before heading out the door to visit his next patient. Tears flowed from Lily's eyes as she slumped over her uncle's bed and rested her head next to his lifeless arm.

And then one day, as Lily and her parents entered Stella and Walter's apartment, they were greeted with the sight they had almost stopped hoping for. Willi was awake, propped up into a sitting position with pillows piled behind his head and back. Meckie was there as always, panting happily this time. Stella had prepared some soup, and Willi was sipping it. He smiled faintly at his niece.

"Welcome back," Lily said, nearly jumping up and down with excitement.

"I think, somewhere in the back of my mind, I could hear your voice," said Willi. He was still so weak that Lily had to bend close to hear him whisper.

"I knew it!" she said. "Everyone told me that you wouldn't hear me. But I knew that you would."

"Thanks," said Uncle Willi. "I think you really helped me."

Lily beamed. It was one more miracle for their family – one that felt huge.

Chapter 26

The bombing continued for several more weeks, keeping Lily and the ghetto residents in a constant state of high alert. First the sirens would begin to blast, signaling the approach of the bomber pilots. Everyone would freeze, wondering if the bombs were going to explode on top of them. Once the all-clear siren blared, residents could take a deep sigh of relief and continue to go about their business. During the first few weeks of their arrival at the Kadoorie School, the siren sounded so often that Lily's parents didn't let her out of their new home, or even out of their sight. But eventually, Lily begged to go outside.

"It's so boring to spend every single minute inside the school," she pleaded. It was fine to be able to play with her friends in the hallways, but Lily longed to be in the open air, roaming the streets of the ghetto as she had always done. "Please let me go out. I promise I'll be careful."

Mom and Pop exchanged weary glances and finally gave in to her persistent pleas. After all, the Kadoorie School was no more protected than any other part of Hongkew, and Lily was probably as safe outside as she was inside. Pop had one last instruction for her as she headed out the door.

"If the siren goes off, just drop to the ground," he told her. "Don't try to run for cover. Stay where you are."

With that promise made, Lily bolted out of the school to go for a walk with Susie. It was a clear day in early August, and even though the heat was stifling, Lily could at least enjoy the blue sky. The girls made their way to an open field on the outskirts of Hongkew. They scavenged for anything that had been dumped there and might be of value. Other people were in the field as well, trying to salvage bits of wood and debris that had been discarded after the bombing. Mice and rats appeared out of nowhere, chasing each other in what was almost a game of tag. With so much less food in the ghetto, the mice were becoming bolder, and there seemed to be more of them than ever.

As Lily and Susie picked their way across the dusty turf, they were suddenly startled by the wail of the sirens, warning of approaching bombers. It was the signal everyone dreaded. The noise of the alarms was deafening; a high-pitched wail coming from loudspeakers that dotted the street poles and buildings. All around the girls, people began to run from the field, holding their hands over their heads, as if that would somehow protect them. Susie grabbed Lily's hand, wanting to join the crowd and head for some kind of shelter.

"Let's get out of here," Susie shouted above the scream of the sirens.

Lily's feet remained firmly planted on the ground. As much as she, too, wanted to run for cover, she knew that was not necessarily the best thing to do. She remembered the kitchen building that had collapsed with so many people inside, not to mention her SACRA, which had been sliced in half – and she remembered her promise to Pop.

"What are you waiting for?" screamed Susie, as she yanked on Lily's arm.

Lily pulled back, hard. "Get down, Susie. We've got to get on the ground."

With a strength she didn't know she possessed, Lily pulled Susie down to her knees, and then pushed her, face down, into the dirt. Then she fell to the ground next to her friend. The two girls covered their heads with their arms and waited.

The sirens continued to scream, and now, the slow rumble of approaching airplane engines joined them. The engines grew louder and more deafening until Lily thought that they were practically on top of them. Her heart pounded, almost keeping time with the pulse of the engines. She covered her ears and prayed that Pop's instructions to stay in one place would prove to be correct. Susie reached out, found Lily's hand, and clutched it tightly. Lily returned the squeeze.

And then, Lily began to sense that the bombers were passing over them and disappearing. The rumble of airplane engines moved farther away. In the distance, there was a high-pitched whistling sound, and Lily felt the earth below her tremble slightly as bombs exploded. But nothing fell close to them. The airplanes had dropped their explosives in another part of Shanghai. Hongkew was safe this time, and so were Lily and Susie.

It was still some time before the girls lifted their heads and looked around. A man lay in the dirt several feet away from Lily. At first, she was afraid he might be dead. But he suddenly lifted his head and stared at the girls. A slow smile spread across his face.

"You don't have to be scared," he said. "They're not going to do anything."

Lily frowned. *How does he possibly know that?* The Americans had dropped bombs on them once before, so what would stop them from doing it again? She stood and pulled Susie up with her. Then she stared at her friend and burst out laughing. Susie's face was covered in dust from the top of her forehead to the tip of her chin. It was as if someone had painted her with white chalk. "You look like one of those *kabuki* dancers," she finally blurted. She had seen pictures of Japanese dancers with their faces painted in thick white make-up.

Susie smiled back. "You should talk," she responded. "Your mother would be frightened to look at you, right now."

"Let's get out of here," Lily said between bursts of laughter. "I think I'll be happy to play indoors for a while."

Mom and Pop were waiting anxiously for Lily when she finally walked into the school. Lily explained that she and Susie had been caught in the open field when the sirens went off. "I did exactly what you told me to do, Pop," she said. "Susie and I didn't run. We just lay flat on the ground and waited for the planes to pass."

Her father nodded, approvingly. "There were no hits on the ghetto, this time. And I don't think Hongkew will be attacked again. But the Americans are not letting up. I think we're going to be hearing that siren a lot more from now on."

Pop was right. Over the next few days, there were repeated air strikes from the skies over Shanghai and other parts of China. No more bombs fell on Hongkew, though that never stopped Lily from dropping to the ground whenever she heard the air raid sirens begin to wail. And then, Pop began to talk about a different kind of explosive that he had heard about.

"The Americans have been working on a bomb that uses atomic energy," he said one afternoon as Lily and her parents sat on their beds eating the lunch they had collected from the food line. Today, it was steamed rice and black beans – not very appetizing, but at least it filled Lily's stomach.

She paused between bites of her meal and looked up. "What is that, Pop?" she asked.

"A new kind of warfare," he replied. "These new bombs are attached to parachutes and they explode in the air. I don't fully understand how they work. But they are bigger and more powerful than any bomb that's ever been developed. And they're meant to destroy everything below them for many miles. Don't worry," he said quickly, noting the instant looks of panic on the faces of Lily and her mother. "The Americans will not make the mistake of dropping those bombs in Shanghai. They are reserving them for Japan. And believe me," he added, "if the Americans drop atomic bombs on Japan, they will put an instant stop to this war in the Pacific. I think we may even be able to see the flames from here."

As her Mom and Pop continued talking, Lily quickly finished up her lunch. She ran down the stairs, passing Harry who looked at her curiously as she bolted by him.

"I'll explain later," she called over her shoulder as she headed out the doors of the Kadoorie School and onto the sidewalk.

Once outside, Lily stood and looked up at the sky. It was a hazy day, almost as cloudy as the day the bombs had first fallen on the Hongkew ghetto. But that's not what she was looking at. Pop had said that if the Americans dropped an atomic bomb on Japan, you would be able to see the flames all the way over here in Shanghai. And that would be the signal that the war in the Pacific had ended. Lily peered upward, straining to spot anything in the sky that resembled a flame. Thick mist spread across the horizon. A few birds floated by on a breeze, disappearing in and out of the cloud cover. But that was it. She sighed deeply and turned to go back inside the school, knowing she would have to wait longer for the war to be over.

Chapter 27

August, 1945

It turned out that Lily did not have to wait as long as she thought for the events that would bring an end to the war in the Pacific. On August 6, 1945, just three weeks after the bombing of Hongkew, the United States dropped its first atomic bomb on a Japanese city called Hiroshima. The bomb was called Little Boy, a code name that referred to the fact that the bomb was shaped like a slim tube. Three days later, on August 9, the United States dropped a second even bigger atomic bomb on the city of Nagasaki. This one was code-named Fat Man. All the Jewish families inside the Kadoorie School were gathered around the shortwave radio the night that President Truman of the United States delivered the news.

We won the race of discovery [for the atomic bomb] against the Germans. We have used its power to shorten the agony of war in order to save the lives of thousands and thousands of...soldiers. We shall continue to use it until we completely destroy Japan's power to create war. Only Japanese surrender will stop us.[6]

President Truman went on to say that Japan had begun the war at Pearl Harbor and now the Americans were going to finish it in Hiroshima and Nagasaki.

Lily shuddered as she heard the broadcast. As terrifying as the bombs in Hongkew had been, there was something even more frightening about these new atomic weapons that had exploded in Japan. Pop had said that he didn't completely understand their power, but that they could wipe out everything in their path. That meant not only buildings and military bases, but people; men, women, and children who would be helpless against the force of this weapon. The American president had said that this atomic bomb was two thousand times more powerful than any weapon that had been used to date. Lily had prayed for the end of the war for as long as she could remember. But was it worth the massive destruction that this kind of bomb could produce? When Lily asked this question of her parents, no one could really answer her. Pop simply shook his head and said, "It will mean our freedom, Lily. And the freedom of all the Jewish refugees here in Hongkew. And it's better that the Americans have this power than the

Nazi or the Japanese army," he added. Lily was still not sure.

The news reports continued to pour in over the next few days.

The United States calls for the unconditional surrender of Japan.
There will be no slowing of efforts until peace is declared.
Japan's Emperor Hirohito scheduled to surrender.

Everyone in the Kadoorie School remained glued to the radio. Each time one of these reports was broadcast, they would cheer. The men would clap each other on the back and the women would hug. Shouts of approval and excitement echoed through the school halls. "It's just a matter of days," everyone said. "Maybe hours." No one wanted to leave the radio for fear that they would miss the long-awaited announcement – the news that the war was over.

Several days later, on August 15, Lily woke from a deep sleep. She stretched in bed and then rose quickly, wanting to get outside and into the food line before it became too long. It was hard enough to line up day after day for each meal. It was worse if it took hours to get to the front. Mom and Pop were still sleeping. That was unusual for them; they were the ones who were always up before the crack of dawn. But they had stayed awake late into the night, listening to radio reports with other families.

Lily tried to be as quiet as possible, knowing how much her parents needed this added sleep. She would save them places in the food line – maybe even bring their meals to them so they wouldn't have to line up at all. That would be a nice treat. She dressed quickly and ran down the hall toward the doors.

As soon as Lily was outside, she looked up. It was becoming a new habit. She would search the sky for any signs of the flames that Pop had talked about from these new atomic bombs. Some of the recent reports had said that nothing could live within a mile of the point where this weapon had hit; that's how powerful it was. The numbers of casualties that were being reported from Japan were in the tens of thousands. And that was only the beginning. Estimates were that hundreds of thousands of Japanese might have been killed. It still made no sense to Lily that millions of Jews had perished in Europe, thousands of soldiers had died in battle, and now hundreds of thousands of Japanese citizens might have been killed.

It was still early, and the sun was just rising on the horizon. It would be another scorcher of a day. Lily was already feeling the intense heat, and she knew it would only get worse as the day went on. Still no sign of any flames, she noted, as she skipped onto the street and headed for the food line. There was a crowd already gathering, and at first Lily thought that others had risen even earlier than she and had beat her to the line. There would be much less food if she didn't get to the front quickly.

But there was something different about the crowd this morning, and about the energy that Lily could feel on the streets of Hongkew.

Kathy Kacer

Jewish and Chinese residents were running in all directions. Everyone was talking and laughing and pointing down the alleyways and narrow lanes. The rickshaw drivers were grinning as they ran by.

Lily spotted Susie charging up the road in her direction.

"Did you hear?" Susie yelled. The noise on the street was beginning to swell along with the growing number of people.

"Hear what?"

"They've surrendered! The Japanese have surrendered!" Susie was laughing and talking so fast that Lily could barely understand what she had just said. She stood in one spot, with her mouth wide open, staring at her friend. Susie finally twirled Lily around and pointed down the street. "Take a good look around," Susie shouted. "What do you see?"

Lily gazed long and hard at the growing crowd of people. Aside from the fact that everyone looked so happy, it was hard, at first, to notice anything different. And then it hit her. There were no Japanese police patrolling on the streets of Hongkew, demanding to see identification papers. There was no guard at the end of East Yuhang Road, keeping people from walking where they wanted. The barbed wire that had blockaded the end of the street was gone! The open road practically called out to Lily and all the Jewish refugees of Hongkew, beckoning them to leave the ghetto and cross into the free part of Shanghai for the first time in years. And when Lily looked around, she realized that the Japanese flag no longer flew from every lamppost

230

and every building. The flags, along with the Japanese patrols and barricades, had all disappeared.

Lily turned to Susie and a slow smile began to creep across her face. The war was over. Liberation day had arrived. They were all finally free.

After the war ended, Lily (far left) attended the
Shanghai Jewish School back in Frenchtown.

Afterword

The Hongkew ghetto was officially liberated on September 3, 1945, when American troops finally began to appear on the streets. They were greeted as heroes by both the Chinese residents and the Jewish refugees. They brought ice cream for Lily and the other children in the ghetto and they had kind and friendly faces. In the following days, there were celebrations everywhere in Hongkew. Blue-and-white Star of David flags were raised across the ghetto. People poured onto the streets to dance and parade and cheer. Freedom had finally arrived and everyone rejoiced in that sweet feeling.

Lily and her family set about planning where and how they were going to live. The Kadoorie School had been a temporary shelter and it was time to find a new apartment. Eventually, Lily's father found a place for the family. It was still just one room, though it was slightly bigger than the one in which they had lived upon first moving to Hongkew. Unfortunately, this apartment had those dreaded bucket toilets that had to be emptied each day by the Chinese coolies who came by with their carts, dripping brown, smelly waste. The family lived there for only a short time before Pop found them a new apartment on top of a store, complete with flush toilets, a deep bathtub, and a kitchen!

Lily and her parents remained in Shanghai for several more years after the war ended. During that time, Mom and Pop went back

After the war, Lily and her family were able to take vacations to the Chinese countryside. That's Lily in the pool at the bottom of the photo.

to work, and Lily attended the Shanghai Jewish School, which was located in Frenchtown where they had lived upon first arriving. Lily traveled there every day on a "school bus" which was really just an open truck with benches facing each other in the back. Many of Lily's friends, including Susie, went as well. Lily and her parents also began to travel in China, taking trips and vacations to the countryside together. Food was more plentiful, thanks to the American soldiers and the Jewish relief groups that provided supplies. Life began to feel somewhat normal.

But in the months following the end of the war, the full details of the Holocaust in Europe began to reach the Jews of Shanghai. Lists with names of individuals who had perished in the death camps, were posted on walls of buildings, including the synagogue. The refugees would rush to read the names on the boards and then collapse on the street as they realized that parents, siblings, cousins, aunts, uncles, and friends were all dead. The jubilant mood that had followed the liberation of Hongkew was replaced with the devastating sadness that this news brought. While the Jews who were imprisoned in the Shanghai ghetto had endured many difficulties during the war, they began to understand how much more their friends and family members had suffered back in Europe. Lily and her family never forgot how incredibly lucky they had been that they and their relatives had managed to escape and stay together during this time.

Within a few years of the end of the war, Jewish families began to

To Lilain When rocks and hills
divide us
And you no more I see
Just take a pen and pencil
And write few lines to me
From your
class-mate
Mabel Cohen 8th December 1947
Shanghai
China
S. J. S.

Many of Lily's friends signed her special autograph book.

Dear Lilian,
If you look
Though this book
In future time
Reading this ryme
Remember mine.
Shanghai Feb 25th 1948
From your friend
Susie Stern

Dear Lily,

True friends are like diamonds,
Precious and rare.
False friends are like autumn leaves,
Scattered everywhere.

Jan. 17th 1948
Shanghai
China

From your friend
Daisy Blum

make plans to leave Shanghai. Some wanted to return to their homes in Europe. Others wanted to start new lives abroad in countries such as Canada, the United States, England, and Australia. Susie and her family left Shanghai, first for Israel and then for Vienna, where they wanted to try to rebuild their lives. Eventually, Susie ended up in England where she lives to this day. She married and has three children and five grandchildren. Susie and Lily continue to be in touch.

Harry and his family received visas to go to Australia. Lily has had no contact with him since that time.

Nini and Poldi left Shanghai when they received papers to allow them to go to Canada. They settled in Toronto where Poldi had a cousin. With them were their two young children, a daughter named Vivian, who had been born in Hongkew just after the end of the war, and a baby boy, born in Guam on the way from Shanghai to Toronto.

Willi married after the war ended. Lily's newest aunt was the young girl named Susi, whom Willi had met in the ghetto. Lily was a bridesmaid at their wedding, which was held in the Ohel Moshe Synagogue, the place where the Jews of the Shanghai ghetto had worshipped during the war.

By 1948, Lily and her parents realized that they needed to leave Shanghai. China was becoming unstable once again. A new kind of political rule called Communism was beginning to take root in Shanghai where the Communist Chinese Army was about to take control. By this time, American diplomats and government officials

After the war, Lily was thrilled when her Uncle Willi married a young woman named Susi. Willi and his bride are pictured in the center. Lily is in front of the bride. Her best friend, Susie Stern is in front of the groom.

had pulled out of Shanghai, and jobs were becoming scarce for non-Chinese people. New rules and restrictions were being imposed by this new Communist government. It was time for Lily and her parents to find a new country in which to live. They wanted to go to Canada to join Nini and Poldi. Mother Lawler, their friend from the Missionary Home, even wrote a letter supporting their application for papers to be able to leave Shanghai. But the only visas they could get were ones to South America. They accepted these and left Shanghai in late 1948.

It was with a mixture of emotions that Lily and her parents sailed away from Shanghai onboard a big ship much like the one that had brought them there ten years earlier. This city had allowed them to enter at a time when few other countries in the world had offered the same refuge. And while life in Shanghai had been harsh, they had survived when so many of their friends who were left behind in Europe had not. For that, Lily's family would be eternally grateful. But the truth was, Shanghai was never the city that Lily and her family would have chosen as a home, were it not for the war that had forced them out of Austria. The Jews of Europe and the Chinese citizens of Shanghai had become unlikely allies in a tough and long struggle that was finally over. It was time for Lily to say good-bye to Shanghai and look ahead to a new chapter in her life.

En route to South America, Lily and her parents stopped in Toronto to visit with Nini and Poldi. They never left Toronto and eventually became citizens of Canada. Stella and Walter along with

Lily brought this hand-painted leather piece with her to Canada when she left Shanghai.

Willi and his wife, Susi, eventually joined them. Lily's family opened a grocery business in the city, and later bought a farm north of Toronto. Lily's parents had another child in 1952; a beloved brother for Lily named Ronnie. Lily finished school and in 1958, she met and married Jimmy Lash who had survived the Holocaust in the Lodz Ghetto of Poland and then in the Auschwitz concentration camp. Lily and Jimmy still live in Toronto and have two children and two grandchildren. Sadly, Ronnie passed away in 2009.

Lily felt a mixture of emotions when she and her family sailed
away from Shanghai in 1948, heading for South America.

Lily Toufar Lash still lives in Toronto. She and her husband have two children and two grandchildren.

In 1988, Lily traveled back to Shanghai for her first and only visit since the end of the war. It was a brief trip, but she was able to see what was left of the Hongkew ghetto. She found the spot where the SACRA had once stood. She was also able to find the Shanghai Jewish School that she attended after the war.

Today, much of the evidence of the Jewish life that existed in Hongkew during the war has disappeared. There are some buildings left standing where thousands of refugees lived during that time, though most of them are in terrible disrepair – even worse than when they housed the Jewish refugees. In recent years, the Ohel Moshe Synagogue has been restored and is now the Shanghai Jewish Refugees Museum. It is filled with photographs and artefacts that document the story of the Jewish refugees who traveled to Shanghai during the war and found a safe haven. There is also a monument in Huoshen Park in Hongkew that is dedicated to the Jewish refugees like Lily who lived there. Survivors of the Shanghai ghetto live around the world, and to this day, many refer to Shanghai as their "Noah's Ark," a place that took them in when few other countries were willing to do the same.

Acknowledgments

I've wanted to write a story about the Shanghai Ghetto for years. It had always seemed remarkable to me that this city housed so many Jewish refugees at a time when few other places around the world were willing to do the same. But I needed to find the right person, one whose Shanghai story I could represent in a book. I was thrilled and lucky to find Lily Toufar Lash.

Lily is a delight. She is smart, spirited, and funny as well as warm, hospitable, and kind. It's been a joy to get to know her, and I have loved every minute we have spent together. Thank you, Lily for the food and flowers that always greeted me. And thank you for enduring my endless questions and opening up your memory vault! You made this project a labor of love. Thanks also to Lily's husband, Jimmy, for the interesting conversations, and Lily's daughter, Shari, for her

Author Kathy Kacer visited this monument in
Huoshen Park in Hongkew, dedicated to the Jewish refugees
who lived there during the Second World War.

insights and support. Many of the family photos were taken by Lily's Uncle Willi, and I appreciate the family allowing the use of these wonderful pictures.

Where do I even begin to thank Margie Wolfe of Second Story Press? Margie is a force in the world of publishing – incredibly astute, compassionate, and determined. I am grateful beyond words for the partnership that we have developed in the creation of my eight books with SSP, and I look forward to many more. I would not have the writing career I have today were it not for Margie.

This was my first opportunity to work with Kathryn Cole as editor. Kathryn has a keen eye for the important elements of a good story and she pushed me to bring out those critical details in this book. It's always a bit anxiety provoking to open up one's work to a new editor. But Kathryn made this experience comfortable and enriching.

Thanks as always to Carolyn Jackson, with her fine attention to detail, for picking up the editing baton from Kathryn and carrying the book through to its completion. Thanks also to Emma Rodgers – marketing guru, and to Phuong Truong and Melissa Kaita. You are all wonderful.

Special thanks to my friend, Joel Gotlieb for introducing me to Lily and to my neighbor, Cecilia Siu and her son Michael for helping with the translation of some Chinese documents.

Finally, and always, to my family and friends. To Rose who is my best buddy for life, to my "ladies" who labored over titles with me, to the Dennills, Kagans, Epsteins, Adlers, and their offspring who enrich my life in so many ways. And to my wonderful husband, Ian Epstein, and my children, Gabi Epstein and Jake Epstein, I love you and cherish your love and laughter in return.

Footnotes

[1] http://www.historyplace.com/speeches/fdr-infamy.htm

[2] Ross, James R., *Escape to Shanghai: A Jewish Community in China,* p. 175, The Free Press, New York, 1994.

[3] Ross, James R., *Escape to Shanghai: A Jewish Community in China,* p. 205, The Free Press, New York, 1994. Print

[4] http://www.jewishmag.com/140mag/holocaust_refugee_ shanghai/holocaust_refugee_shanghai.htm

[5] http://www.army.mil/d-day/message.html

[6] http://www.youtube.com/watch?v=e9_d14YRvIU

Photo Credits

Cover photos courtesy Lily Lash and the family of Willi Karpel

page ii: courtesy Lily Lash and the family of Willi Karpel

page 5: courtesy Lily Lash and the family of Willi Karpel

page 7: courtesy Lily Lash and the family of Willi Karpel

page 7, right: © Christian Kadluba

page 16, both: courtesy Lily Lash and the family of Willi Karpel

page 32: courtesy Lily Lash and the family of Willi Karpel

page 48-49: United States Holocaust Memorial Museum (USHMM), courtesy of Ralph Harpuder

page 52: courtesy Lily Lash and the family of Willi Karpel

page 53: courtesy Lily Lash and the family of Willi Karpel

page 65: © Yad Vashem

page 74: USHMM, courtesy of Eric Goldstaub

page 75: USHMM, courtesy of Eric Goldstaub

page 91: courtesy Lily Lash and the family of Willi Karpel

page 100-101: USHMM, courtesy of Ralph Harpuder

page 106: courtesy Lily Lash and the family of Willi Karpel

page 113: courtesy Lily Lash and the family of Willi Karpel

page 118, both: courtesy Lily Lash and the family of Willi Karpel

page 120: USHMM, courtesy of Ralph Harpuder

page 124: USHMM Beit Hatfutsot Comite International de la Croix Rouge YIVO Institute for Jewish Research, courtesy of Ernest G. Heppner Yair Hendl

page 125: courtesy Lily Lash and the family of Willi Karpel

page 141: © Yad Vashem

page 149: courtesy Lily Lash and the family of Willi Karpel

page 161: USHMM, courtesy of Mary Catalina (Siegmund Sobel collection)

page 193: USHMM, courtesy of Ernest G. Heppner

page 193, inset: USHMM Museum Beit Hatfutsot Comite International de la Croix Rouge YIVO Institute for Jewish Research, courtesy of Ernest G. Heppner Yair Hendl

page 232 - 242: courtesy Lily Lash and the family of Willi Karpel

page 244: © Kathy Kacer

page 249: author photo by Negin Sairafi

About the Author

KATHY KACER has written many books about the Holocaust, including eight other books in the Holocaust Remembrance Series for Young Readers: *We Are Their Voice: Young People Respond to the Holocaust*, *The Secret of Gabi's Dresser*, *The Night Spies*, *Clara's War*, *The Underground Reporters*, *Hiding Edith*, *The Diary of Laura's Twin*, and *To Hope and Back*. A former psychologist, Kathy has traveled around the world speaking to young people about the importance of remembering the Holocaust. She also addresses adults about how to teach sensitive material to young children. In 2010 she published her first book for adults: *Restitution: A family's fight for their heritage lost in the Holocaust*. Kathy lives in Toronto with her family.

Visit Kathy's website and blog at www.kathykacer.com

The Holocaust Remembrance Series for Young Readers

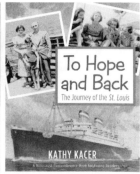

We Are Their Voice
Young People Respond to the Holocaust
Kathy Kacer
ISBN: 978-1-897187-96-8
$14.95

To Hope and Back
Kathy Kacer
ISBN: 978-1-897187-96-8
$14.95

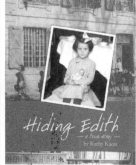

Guardian Angel House
Kathy Clark
ISBN: 978-1-897187-58-6
$14.95

The Diary of Laura's Twin
Kathy Kacer
ISBN: 978-1-897187-39-5
$14.95

Hana's Suitcase
Karen Levine
ISBN: 978-1-896764-55-9
$16.95

Hiding Edith — *A True Story*
Kathy Kacer
ISBN: 978-1-897187-06-7
$14.95

The Underground Reporters
A True Story
Kathy Kacer
ISBN:
978-1-896764-85-6
$15.95

The Righteous Smuggler
Debbie Spring
ISBN:
978-1-896764-97-9
$9.95

Clara's War
Kathy Kacer
ISBN:
978-1-896764-42-9
$8.95

The Secret of Gabi's Dresser
Kathy Kacer
ISBN:
978-1-896764-15-3
$7.95

The Night Spies
Kathy Kacer
ISBN:
978-1-896764-70-2
$8.95